IMAGES

SONJA HENIE 1912–1969

PERFORMED

Henie Onstad

Images Performed
Sonja Henie (1912–1969)

Editor: Gunhild Varvin
Editorial staff: Martine Hoff Jensen
Copy Editor: Evy Fjøren
Design: Non-Format/ANTI
Typography: Post Grotesk by Josh Finklea and
Sonja Display by Non-Format/ANTI
Paper: Munken Print Cream, Galerie Art Gloss White,
Munken Kristall and JAC Brillant
Print: Göteborgstryckeriet
Published by: Henie Onstad Kunstsenter
and Forlaget Press

Henie Onstad Kunstsenter
Sonja Henies vei 31
1311, Høvikodden, Norge
www.hok.no
ISBN: 978-82-328-0444-3

©2021 Henie Onstad Kunstsenter,
Forlaget Press and the authors
First published in Norway in 2021
Copies: 1000
Artworks: 35
Cover: Sonja Henie, St Mortiz, 1928.
Photo: Henie Onstad archives / NTB

Every effort has been to acknowledge
correct copyright of images where applicable.
Any error or omissions are unintentional
and should be brought to the attention of
Henie Onstad Kunstsenter, which will arrange
for corrections to appear in any reprint.

Henie Onstad

press

→

Foundation stone

Sonja Henie donated her art collection, prizes and fortune in order to create the Henie Onstad Kunstsenter. Her wish was for it to be a place where art happens and visitors can experience contemporary art.
On Midsummer's Eve in 1967, she laid the foundation stone at Høvikodden. Her husband Niels Onstad stands behind her while she makes a speech. Photo: Henie Onstad archive.

Foreword

Publishing a book about Sonja Henie is like diving into a treasure trove of myths, stories and performances. It has involved the study of a large amount of richly detailed visual material. The goal of the book is to give an insight into Sonja Henie's intense passion for her own age – and for posterity. Our wish is to show her as an athlete, businesswoman, collector and patron of the arts. Not only is Sonja Henie a historical celebrity, she was and still is a role model for many. Henie was very conscious of her own public persona. She created the face she showed the world and was extremely aware of the marketing value of the pose.

Sonja Henie's tireless energy laid the foundation for the Henie Onstad Kunstsenter. She was one of Norway's first and biggest female collectors of art. With her experience from showbusiness and the historical tradition of patrons of the arts from the United States, she laid the foundation for the institution that we currently manage for a broad audience. As a businesswoman, Henie secured the institution's finances while managing her own. She developed friendships with artists who shared her temperament, and it was she, not her husband, who steered the Henie Onstad collection in a contemporary direction.

In addition to what she has left us, Sonja Henie's life also opens the door to ethical questions related to the public lives of child stars who are pushed towards extraordinary achievements and fame. In this way, the story of her life offers a good example of how far it is wise to go to please an audience, no matter whether one's motivations are idealistic, or about winning, making money and building a brand. Sonja Henie's story is also important because it shows how long it takes to be forgiven for one's mistakes.

Sonja Henie was a product of the times in which she lived. She was shaped by those times, but as a prominent and outspoken individual, she also defied them.

As director of the institution for which she laid the foundation, I am grateful for her legacy and all the opportunities it continues to provide, far beyond what she and Niels Onstad could have imagined.

Henie Onstad thanks the writers, photographers and ANTI for their contributions to this book.

Tone Hansen
Director, Henie Onstad Art Center

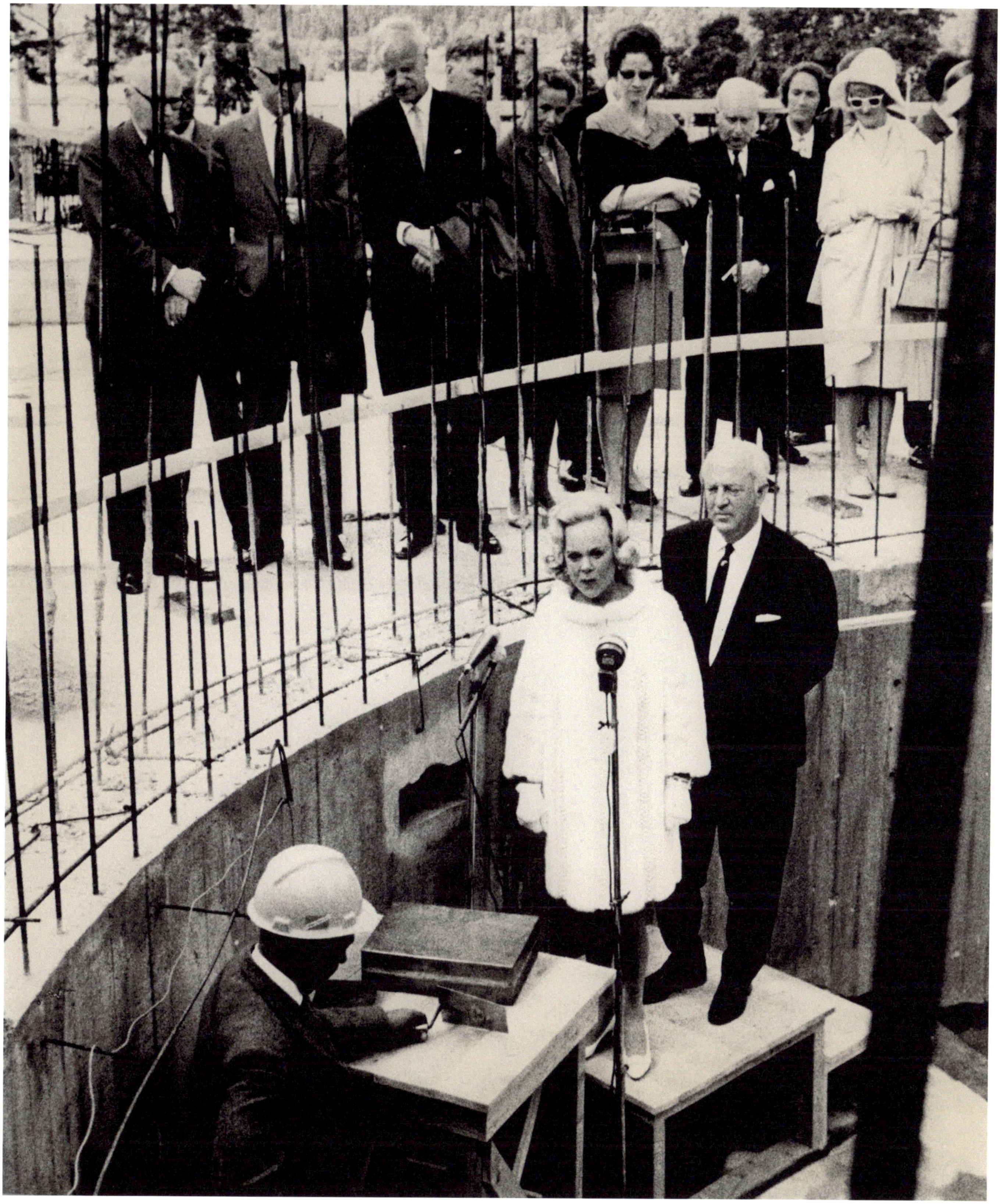

WHAT REMAINS

Text: Gunhild Varvin

Much is still written about Sonja Henie, and news clips featuring her name appear regularly in media coverage of the museum Henie Onstad Kunstsenter. Not only was she the undisputed Norwegian champion who laid the foundation for figure skating as we know it today, she also made a film career in Hollywood, became one of the world's very first glamorous superstars, toured the world with her huge ice shows, and made her mark as an art collector. Sonja Henie's fame allows us to interpret her life through photographs and press clippings. This book is based on Høvikodden's visual archive, which was passed on by Sonja Henie herself. Her story is illuminated by chapters written by a number of writers with their own perspectives.

The Skater

From little girl to middle-aged woman, Sonja Henie was always training with her skates on. She defined figure skating as we know it today and broke new ground for women in professional sports. Hasse Farstad, former head of the Skating Museum and Oslo Skating Club and board member of the Norwegian Skating Association, has written about how Henie trained, won and helped create the sport of figure skating as we know it today.

The Brand

There is still a lot to learn from Sonja Henie's ability to refine and be true to her talent, constantly making the effort, winning and being in control. She was not afraid to think big, to wish on the brightest of stars – hoping to become one herself. By using her own physique and her personal story, and by being generous in inviting the press into her home, she laid the ground for several businesses and a fictional universe based on her own persona.
The chapter on her brand is written by me, Gunhild Varvin, on the basis of questions that have been raised throughout a decade of working as a press contact and being responsible for the marketing of Henie Onstad.

Cuba

Henie's ability to seize the spirit of the times, to incorporate novelty and create whole performances inspired by what she saw and heard is highlighted by Martine Hoff Jensen from Henie Onstad Kunstsenter. With a background as a journalist, Hoff Jensen writes about the Cuban elements in the performance Henie toured with when she visited Oslo and Jordal Arena in 1953. Having spoken to the dancer Marta Castillo, Hoff Jensen writes about how the dancers viewed Sonja Henie as boss. At the same time, she highlights Henie's anxiety about returning to Norway in 1953 after many years abroad.

Art

Sonja Henie learned to appreciate contemporary European art when she met her third husband, Niels Onstad (1909–1978). Henie was quick and straight to the point, even when collecting art. The first pictures were incorporated into the foundation in 1963 with the next ones being transferred in the years that followed. Caroline Ugelstad is chief curator at Henie Onstad and reveals how Henie created the collection while drawing the historical framework of the time in which she was operating.

Architecture

The art centre at Høvikodden was the last of Sonja Henie's creations. Its form reflects Henie's well-known pirouettes on the ice, her assured touch, ambition and ability to bring international trends back to Norway. Professor of architecture Erik Fenstad Langdalen sheds light on the largest monument she left us, illuminating the final years of her life with a professional analysis. She had a keen eye for which works of art she purchased; she also sat on the committees that laid the foundation for the architectural competitions, participated in the subsequent processes and took on the post of chairwoman of the art centre's board.

Images Performed

By studying the images we find of her today, we see how boldly and professionally she performs her own image and takes a natural place at the forefront. She does not stand behind her husband. She stands in front of him or next to him. In the press clippings, she speaks as naturally as her husband, and when it comes to photo shoots, she plays on her own very special experience.

The signed portraits she collected are presented in a separate chapter. She was surrounded by heads of state, movie stars and sporting legends throughout her life. Greetings from people like Robert Kennedy, Ingrid Bergman, Charlie Chaplin, Adolf Hitler, Trygve Lie and Walt Disney reveal her spectacular network. For better and for worse, this whole cast of characters is part of her story.

It is difficult to find Sonja Henie's own texts in the official archives. On the other hand, we find her voice in personal letters to Niels Onstad. The letters were not written with a view to being made public, but some of them are nevertheless included in the book to shed light on her life and the fantastic pace and the infinite details she was in charge of on her many tours.

The book is not intended to be a new biography of Sonja Henie. The texts are based on and inspired by the places that bear her name, the things she did and left behind, the forms she created and the museum that stands as a testimony to her.

←

Mythologies

Sonja Henie grew up in Oslo and mythical stories were associated with her from early childhood. “She was born in an incredible winter storm in mid-April as a foreshadowing of her future skating career,” and she was named Sonja after an artist friend of her father Wilhelm Henie said “it was a name that would sound good in public.” Here is Sonja at three years old with her big brother Leif, five years older than her. Photo: Henie Onstad archive.

→

No. 1

By the age of twenty, Sonja Henie had managed to become Olympic figure skating champion twice in a row, in 1928 and in 1932, and did not give up until she took Olympic gold a third time in 1936. Photo: Henie Onstad archive.

←

Frogner

Selma Henie, Sonja Henie's mother, was half Irish and remained by her daughter's side throughout her life, even when she was negotiating big Hollywood deals. When Sonja was four years old, the Henie family moved from Bankplassen in central Oslo to 52 Thomas Heftyes gate in Frogner. From there it was a short route to Frogner ice rink and Per Aabel's ballet school. Photo: Henie Onstad archive.

→

Ambition

Training took precedence over schooling and early in her primary education she was taken out of school to focus fully on skating. Sonja Henie's early childhood was documented through professional photographs which show that she belonged to Oslo's upper middle class at the beginning of the twentieth century. Photo: Wilse/Henie Onstad archive.

↑

The family business

The whole family got involved in Sonja's skating career. The prime mover was her father Wilhelm, well supported by her mother Selma. Big brother Leif helped as a business partner. From left in the sled: Wilhelm opposite Selma. In the "back seat", Sonja flanked by Leif on her right side and Austrian double Olympic figure skating champion Karl Schäfer. Photo: Henie Onstad archive.

→

Sunday trips

With Oslo as a starting point, Sunday trips were often taken on skis into the woods from Frognerseteren. Sonja spent much of the year at the family cabin, "Hengi", in Finse, training on ice. Here she is with her brother Leif. Photo: Henie Onstad archive.

→

Dogs

The Henie family had several dogs, and as an adult Sonja Henie developed a special interest in Norwegian elkhounds. With houses at Landøya in Asker and on Delfern Drive in LA, she elected to have four elkhounds: two in each country. Photo: Henie Onstad archive.

←

Leisure

Spending time on vacation, leisure and recreation were relatively new concepts in the early 1900s. With a summer house at Landøya, summers were spent on the fjord. After the Henie family moved to the United States in 1936, the house at Landøya became the family's "anchor" in Norway. Photo: Henie Onstad archive.

→

Wilhelm Henie (1872–1937)

As a businessman (furs and bicycles) and a prize-winning athlete with a gold at the 1894 cycling world championships and a silver at the 1896 European skating championships, father Wilhelm was Sonja Henie's first coach and manager. He loved speed and was one of the first people to own a car in Norway. For several years he also drove the fastest boat on the Oslo fjord. Photo: Henie Onstad archive.

→

Landøya

In her autobiography *My Life's Adventures* (1953), Sonja Henie wrote that the summer house in Asker belonged to her father more than anyone else. It was there he gathered his friends and gave Sonja and her brother some unforgettable summer holidays. Here, Sonja is on the pier in 1929, the year before she toured America and ice skated for a packed Madison Square Garden in New York. Photo: Henie Onstad archive.

→

Outfits and the show

With a father who was a fur dealer and a mother who could sew, Sonja performed in specially designed outfits from the very beginning. The details were often made of leather. Here in Vienna, 1924. Photo: Henie Onstad archive.

←

19 February 1927

Sonja Henie was 14 years old when she represented Norway in the world championships at Frogner Stadium. It was here that she became world champion for the first time. Photo: Henie Onstad archive.

←

Exhibition

Parallel with competitions, Sonja Henie held many skating exhibitions. In addition to her sporting achievements, she learned early on to include numbers and poses that captivated audiences and the media. Here she is appearing for the press in Vienna in 1924. Photo: Henie Onstad archive.

THE SKATER

Sonja Henie is a legend in the sport of figure skating. Not only did she win nineteen international gold medals, including three Olympic gold medals as an amateur, she also became the biggest star the world had ever seen in professional skating.

Text: Hasse Farstad

Some aspects of Sonja Henie's early years as an athlete are entirely in keeping with the current formula for success in Norwegian elite sport. One of the central elements is a rounded exposure to sport in childhood and early adolescence.

Henie was a versatile athlete who reached a high level of performance in tennis, swimming, ballet and horse riding. As a 17-year-old in 1929, Sonja Henie reached the semi-finals of the National Tennis Championships and many were of the opinion that she was overlooked as a candidate to receive the prestigious Egeberg Honorary Prize for athletes who excel in more than one sport.

Other parts of Henie's early sporting years are most certainly not in line with today's Norwegian sports model. Under current children's sports regulations, for example, she would not have been permitted to participate in her first figure skating competition – when she won the beginner's classification for skaters under fourteen years of age, she hadn't yet turned ten years old. She was furthermore taken out of school early, during her primary education. Such inadequate schooling and one-sided prioritisation of sports could not be recommended for anyone – not in 1923, and not today.

Sports ambitions trump schooling

In her mother Selma (1884–1961) and father Wilhelm Henie's (1872–1937) defence, language learning quickly became a priority during the child star's extensive travel activities. Sonja Henie learned both German and English at an early stage, and later in life proved that she had a good grasp of mathematics, media and communication.

According to Birger Børjeson (1896–1962), one of the leading Norwegian figure skaters of the time, Sonja Henie could have become a great ballet dancer if she had pursued it. As a child, she began dancing in Oslo with the classical ballet instructor Love Krohn (1892–1951) and with Per Aabel (1902–1999), who was an excellent ballet dancer before becoming an actor. At the beginning of her figure skating career, Sonja Henie also often took classes with the world-famous Russian ballerina Tamara Karsavina (1885–1978) in London.

But Sonja Henie wanted to be and would go on to become a figure skater. Her fundamental fitness, physique and motor skills from other sports activities undoubtedly laid the foundation for the historic heights she achieved on the ice.

Sonja Henie grew up at a time when girls and women were scarcely able to participate in organised sports. Figure skating was one of the first sports to have women's championships, but even there, male athletes had been competing for the title of World Champion for twenty-eight years before women got their first official world championship in 1924.

As a figure skater, Sonja Henie's name is first mentioned in the Oslo Skating Club's (OSC) yearbook for 1922. Henie was a member of the club's figure skating school, which held a competition to close the season at Frogner Stadium on 11 March. She was not yet ten years old, but won the under-14s class with a wide margin of victory between her and the nine other competitors.

To the Olympics as an 11-year-old

The OSC yearbook also tells us that Sonja Henie and other students from the figure skating school held an exhibition during the World Speed skating Championships at Frogner Stadium in February 1922 – a performance that thrilled the sold-out crowd. This would be Henie's first experience of performing for 20,000 spectators.

Her journey rocketed onwards via junior C to international championship skater in the senior classification. Only two years after Henie had been the half-time entertainment during the skating star Harald Strøm's (1897–1977) World Cup triumph, the two of them met as part of the Norwegian squad for the first Winter Olympics, which were being held in Chamonix, France at the end of January 1924.

Here the experienced Harald Strøm was favourite for gold in the 5,000 and 10,000 metres, while 11-year-old Sonja Henie would make her international debut. A superb freestyle skating programme at the National Championships two weeks earlier had won her first prize in the women's classification. She was not named Norwegian champion, however, because her result in the compulsory figure tracing programme failed to satisfy the minimum requirements. Her fellow club member Ingrid Gulbrandsen (1899–1975) became Norwegian champion, but it was Henie who was sent to the Winter Olympics. She thrilled Chamonix with a fantastic special skating programme. She still ended up in last place because she had not mastered the demanding figure skating exercises that were part of the compulsory programme.

The difficult compulsory figures programme

Sonja Henie made her world championship debut on home ground at Frogner Stadium in Oslo in February 1924, in the first official world championship for women. The first world championships for men dated back to 1896. Although women's championships had been held since 1906, the winner of these championships was not named World Champion until 1924. Prior to this, the winners were named ISU champions after the International Skating Union.

In the inaugural event, Herma Szabo-Plank (1902–1986) from Austria, the reigning queen of figure skating, was scored the clear winner by all five judges. Sonja Henie came fifth overall, but in the special programme three judges ranked her second after Szabo-Plank. The other two had her in third and fourth place respectively.

In the special programme the focus is on speed, choreography, pirouettes, jumps, combinations of jumps, steps and leaps. The compulsory programme consists of a set of intricate figure skating exercises in figure eights, three turns, loops and more, where the skaters are judged according to how precisely they balance on the outer and inner edges while skating backwards and forwards and performing countless turns.

In Sonja Henie's time, the compulsory programme counted towards

60 per cent of the final result, while the special programme counted for 40 per cent. Even as an 11-year-old, Henie had made her definitive breakthrough as a special programme skater. At the same time, it was obvious what had to be done to become a genuine champion figure skater: She would have to iron out the kinks in her compulsory figure exercises.

In February 1925, Henie won her first Norwegian Championship title. We discover from OSC's yearbook that she had worked hard on the figures: "Sonja Henie, who had visited Vienna for training, participated for the first time this year and showed that she has made great progress since last year. Her compulsory exercises were considerably better than before, but she can indeed skate these even better. Then, with her impressive special programme, she will likely be in with a chance at the great international championships".

Henie was on the cusp of becoming a major attraction holding exhibitions for large numbers of spectators in Oslo, Hamar, Brandbu, Elverum and Rjukan at the age of twelve. To a great degree, Oslo Skating Club used her performances, and those of other promising figure skaters, as propaganda for the sport.

When Sonja Henie's career took off in earnest, the skating club had the fine idea of arranging "Festivals of Fire" at Frogner Stadium. These celebrations were held to celebrate Henie's triumphs after the major championships. With large crowds, well-organised show programmes and money ringing in the tills, these shows laid a solid foundation for Sonja Henie's magnificent, professional ice shows in the future.

Sonja challenges Austria's skating queen

The following year, at the world championship in Stockholm in February 1926, it became very clear that Jaross-Szabo would now have to keep an eye on the shooting star from Norway. True enough, all the judges scored her ahead of Henie in the compulsory programme, but her points advantage was no longer insurmountable. And when it came to the special programme, there was a "dead heat" between them. Three judges scored them joint first place, while one judge had Jaross-Szabo as the winner and another had Henie as the best-placed. The final result was gold for Jaross-Szabo and silver for Henie – the first of a total of eleven world championship medals.

The OSC yearbook for 1926 states "during the world championships, Sonja Henie displayed such outstanding skating that from now on Norway must be a contender when this championship is contested. Sonja was very well received during the freestyle programme".

That same season, Henie also won her first national championships in pair skating, alongside her more experienced club mate Arne Lie (1903–1978). They followed it up with a victory in the pair skating competition at the world championships in Stockholm. The following weekend, Henie and Lie were sent to the world pair skating championships in Berlin. There they finished in fifth, but still became the hot topic of the championship. Two of the seven judges had them as winners, while one had them in second place. Among the other judges they were ranked, respectively, sixth, seventh, seventh and ninth (second to last!).

German newspapers reported that Henie-Lie's programme and execution appealed to the public. Their skating created overwhelming excitement among the almost 10,000-strong crowd. After the pair finished their programme, the applause was so intense that at least five minutes passed before the next pair could begin. "If the audience could decide, the Norwegian pair would have placed first," the newspapers wrote.

The Austrian Fritz Kachler (1888–1973) was one of the judges who placed Henie-Lie as the winners. After the championship he wrote in the Wiener Sporttagblatt newspaper, "The peak of commotion and applause was reached when little 13-year-old Sonja Henie and her partner Arne Lie performed their programme. This included all the hits with which champion skaters can equip their special figures programme: standing and sitting pirouettes, leaps and moon combinations in unbroken succession."

At the Winter Olympics in St. Moritz in 1928, it was already clear that Sonja Henie would focus on individual skating. This meant that there could be no focus on her pair skating career with Arne Lie, although many believe that these two could have revolutionised the discipline of pair skating. Their energetic, artistic Nordic School is in line with the development of pair skating after the Second World War. In 1951, the ISU introduced a separate new discipline – ice dance – which would involve beautiful, romantic dance movements on ice to a greater extent than pair skating, with its spectacular lifts and jumps, did. Henie-Lie competed in the national championships at Frogner Stadium in 1927 and at Sandefjord Stadium in 1928, and won both with high scores for style.

Sonja Henie also became Norwegian champion in the individual programme at both championships. At Lillehammer Stadium in 1929, she took her fifth individual National Championship title in a row. Henie-Lie did not participate in the pair skating programme here. Training and exhibitions in London, Berlin, Vienna and other figure skating metropolises took too much of her time for it to be a sensible to participate in the Norwegian championships.

Coming out on top at the World Championships

In 1927, Sonja Henie would start her second world championships on home ground at Frogner Stadium – now as the clear favourite, alongside Herma Jaross-Szabo. Until 1927, Hungary, Austria and Germany had completely dominated the sport of women's figure skating. Henie's victory ahead of the Austrian provoked an outcry from these figure skating superpowers. It was a close-fought battle. Among the five judges, three Norwegian judges had Sonja Henie as the winner, while the judges from Austria and Germany thought that Jaross-Szabo had earned her sixth World Championship title. In her 1977 autobiography *Mitt livs eventyr* [*My Life's Adventures*], Henie accurately sums up the background to her first world championship triumph. She clearly had a sense of being robbed of victory by Central European judges in her first international championships, and writes that it was a blessing that the 1927 world championship would take place in an arena "where the judges came under the control of our own audience. I had also grown up, had more strength in my body, and had been training intensively".

Sonja describes the training ahead of her first world championship victory as terrifically hard. For a full six weeks, Henie, her family and support staff lived at an altitude of over 1200 metres in Finse to train at her "private training palace" – the natural ice hall built by the local hotel to attract affluent tourists from Scandinavia and Central Europe. During her training period, her improvised exhibitions attracted significant crowds.

Before the Winter Olympics in St. Moritz, Switzerland in 1928, the solid training work continued, including altitude training in Finse. Henie took the gold both at the Olympics and in the subsequent world championships in London. OSC's yearbook states that all doubts about the "judging scandal" in Oslo the year before were thereby negated: "As we recall, the foreign press attempted to diminish Sonja's championship victory by casting doubts on the Norwegian judging majority. This time the judges came from England, France, Austria, Sweden and Norway."

Unbeatable Henie

After returning from the Olympics and the World Championships, Sonja Henie held an exhibition at Frogner Stadium to benefit the Norwegian Olympic Committee (today known as the Norwegian Confederation of Sports). Among other major events that season were two successful performances in Bergen that attracted a total of 32,000 spectators – even in unusually ice-cold weather conditions.

In the years that followed, Sonja Henie won a new Olympic gold in Lake Placid in the United States in 1932 and won every world championship up to 1936. In 1931, the European figure skating championships were held for the first time, and she won six out of a possible six European championship golds during the same period.

Henie faced numerous obstacles. She overcame the historically dominant Central Europeans' underestimation of a Norwegian figure skating upstart. When Henie made her debut at the Olympics and the world championships in 1924, some questioned why "a child" should be allowed to participate. Eventually she proved herself and mastered the compulsory programme. Since Henie had also become the best in compulsory figures, she constantly had to disprove the notion that her renowned special skating programme would stagnate. She also had to battle the figure skating world's desire to see new stars reach the top. Austria, the United States and Sweden cultivated highly talented and glamorous figure skaters and in these countries there was a burning desire to see their own skaters reach their peak. None of them managed to beat Henie. Eventually, all hopes for a new queen of figure skating were tied to Sonja Henie's retirement – couldn't she move into the movies or a professional career on the ice?

Crucial coaches – and elite sports in the blood

In 1923, Sonja's father Wilhelm Henie hired Stixrud to coach his daughter. That Henie overcame her problems with the compulsory programme, probably had a lot to do with her coach. Henie writes in her biography,

> He always worked towards an ideal, he saw mistakes and he wanted to correct them. He was tireless in his visits to Finse in the early years I was up there training. I admired his mood and his humour, his good-natured way of working. He basically had to coach two of us – my father too. My father also wanted to understand what Stixrud was demanding from each exercise, and when the coach was away, my father would take his place. It was tiring, but today I understand what that work has given me.

Wilhelm Henie knew from his own experience what it took to make one's mark in elite sports. In 1894, he became Norway's first world champion in any sport – in track cycling. He also won a medal at the world speed skating championships.

In her biography, Sonja Henie also highlights her coach Howard Nicholson (1896–1978), who helped her overcome fresh hurdles in the years from 1931 until the Olympics in 1936.

> I met him in Southampton, where he was a figure skating instructor, and both my father and my mother immediately understood that this was a man who could teach us something. Nicholson immediately set up a whole new training programme for me, and it led to nothing less than a revolution in the way I viewed figure skating. After the first season of training, every year we travelled to London to get new inspiration. I had never known such fitness and improvement, and once Nicholson understood that he had a willing pupil, he took a special interest in my skating.

Figure skating as a springboard to Hollywood

Before the 1936 season, Sonja Henie had decided that it would be her last and that gold in the Olympics and the world championships would be the crucial springboard for a career in the movies. She and her father hired Nicholson as her personal coach during the European championships in Berlin, the Olympics in Garmisch-Partenkirchen and the world championships in Paris.

During the Olympics in Garmisch, Henie faced yet another challenge. For the first time, she would be before a panel of judges featuring not a single Norwegian member. It had been expected that OSC's Birger Børjeson would judge, but an error led to no judge from Norway being registered. This season, for the first time in history, open judging would be used in figure skating, meaning the audience and participants would be able to see what score the skaters had received immediately after each performance.

"I trusted the foreigners to judge fairly, and that's what they did," Sonja writes in *My Life's Adventures*.

The Olympics in Garmisch-Partenkirchen in 1936 were planned as a display of propaganda for the German Führer Adolf Hitler and his new Nazi regime. Sonja Henie was one of Hitler's big favourites as an athlete, and when she gave the grandstand the "Sieg Heil" gesture before her performance, she caused a stir. There has been much discussion as to whether there was any political dimension to the gesture. Henie dismissed this speculation. She said on several occasions that her actions were impulsive and not at all political.

The Norwegian figure skating judge Reidar Lund rounds up Sonja Henie's career in OSC's yearbook for 1936, in the form of a graph and table that express her achievements and development in numbers. The graph shows a steadily rising line, culminating at the 1936 world championship in Paris, with Henie achieving 95 per cent of the available points. During the world championship at Frogner Stadium ten years earlier, she had achieved 87 per cent of the maximum points.

Still an elite athlete in film and shows

Following 19 gold medals – ten in the world championships, six in the European championships and three in the Olympics – her journey took another direction, as planned: onwards to an fairy-tale career in Hollywood and an equally fantastic time as co-owner and prima ballerina in her own professional ice shows.

However, day-to-day life as an elite athlete did not end with her move into movies. The shooting of the long skating scenes were a terrible strain on her physique. For the first time in her career, she took up massage because she skated so far and with such concentration that her muscles ached.

In addition to two demanding film shoots annually, Sonja Henie developed ever new ice shows every year featuring herself in the lead role, and toured all over the United States and large swathes of Europe. Writing in her autobiography about a legendary month of ice shows at Jordal Arena in Oslo in 1953, which was seen by 350,000 spectators (the population of Oslo at the time was 300,000), Henie sums up the decade that had passed since she was asked if her 1943 season touring the United States would be her last:

> In these past ten years I have had a tougher annual schedule than in my competitive career. The audience's demands on the quality of the revues have grown steadily. Beyond the confines of the ice rink, I have several other irons in the fire. Still, my fitness is holding out, as are – thank God – my good spirits.

Sources:

Oslo Skøiteklub, *Year books*, 1922–1936

Oslo Skøiteklub, *150-årsberetning*, 2014

Hasse Farstad, *Articles about figure skating*, Skøytemuseet

Sonja Henie, *Mitt livs eventyr*, Bokhandlerforlaget, 1977

International Skating Union, *75 Years of European and World's Championships in Figure Skating*, 1967

←

Skagen, 1918

The Henie family holidayed in Skagen in the summer of 1918. Six-year-old Sonja stormed to victory in the 100-metre sprint. Photo: Henie Onstad archive.

→

Signed photographs

Sonja Henie handed out signed photographs to friends and fans as special calling cards and gifts. Throughout her life, she used these types of images to build a narrative about herself. At first, photographs like this one were signed for her (probably by her parents). Eventually she did it herself. Photo: Henie Onstad archive.

←

Olympics, January 1924

At eleven years old, Sonja Henie was sent to Chamonix to represent Norway during the world's first Winter Olympics. Despite doing well in several programmes, she ended up in last place. A range of sources do not believe the judges took her seriously. Photo: Henie Onstad archive.

Sonja
12 aar
1925.

→

Oslo Skating Club (OSC)

Sonja Henie went on to skate for OSC, which is still based in Frogner today. In 2021 the Sonja Henie ice hall was opened, giving the team the opportunity to train all year round. In addition to the hall that bears her name, the "Sonja statuette" award was also established. It will be awarded each year for achievements in figure skating. Photo: Henie Onstad archive.

←

But smile

Martin Stixrud was one of Sonja Henie's coaches. He drilled into her: "Be careful, don't forget your schoolwork. The only road to victory is through a solid compulsory programme. And during the competition – smile! Sometimes you might be in pain, but smile anyway." In the picture we see Sonja Henie during the Olympics in 1924. Photo: Henie Onstad archive.

←

The Norwegian hope

The Olympic Committee wanted to refuse to allow 11-year-old Sonja to participate in the 1924 games. A child could turn it into a farce. But Wilhelm Henie stood his ground and saw to it that his daughter was allowed to compete. She came eighth – out of eight participants. In the picture, she is posing with the Swedish figure skater Gillis Grafström. Photo: AP/ Henie Onstad archive.

→

New goals

Sonja Henie continued to compete and do not let up before she had claimed 19 gold medals – ten in the world championships, six in the European championships, and three in the Olympics. Photo: Henie Onstad archive.

↑

The short skirt

As a young girl, it was natural for her to wear short skirts. But unlike her adult competitors, who skated in ankle-length skirts, Sonja Henie let her hem creep higher and higher as she got older. Photo: Henie Onstad archive.

→

Music and ballet

Henie is credited with developing figure skating with music and movements borrowed from ballet. Sonja trained at Per Aabel's ballet school from a young age. Photo: Henie Onstad archive.

↑

Prize collection

Henie appearing with her very first world championship medal in Frogner in 1927. She had already won a whole arsenal of prizes. Two years later, Wilhelm Henie installed an exhibition of her prizes in his fur shop on Prinsens gate. The exhibition attracted a large audience. Photo: Henie Onstad archive.

→

Pair skating

In 1926, Sonja Henie won her first Norwegian championship in pair skating alongside Arne Lie. The image shows the couple in Stockholm during another championship that same year. They won there too. Photo: Dagens Nyheter/ Henie Onstad archive.

Foto:
DAGENS NYHETER

←

Allrounder

Sonja Henie was a versatile athlete who achieved a high level in tennis, swimming, ballet and horse riding. Photo: Henie Onstad archive.

→

The tomboy

Family friend Charles Hoff had a background as an athlete and sports journalist, and coached Sonja Henie in sprinting. He said that Henie would play with the boys in the street as early as the age of two. She loved to fight and did well in many sports, including ski jumping. Photo: Henie Onstad archive.

←

Tennis

As a 17-year-old in 1929, Sonja Henie made it to the semi-finals of the Norwegian tennis championships. Many considered that she was overlooked as a candidate for the prestigious Egeberg Honorary Prize for excelling in more than one sport. Photo: Henie Onstad archive.

←

The photogenic tough nut

Sonja Henie could be called a tough nut of a girl. She was audacious and never complained if she fell. Family friend Charles Hoff called her "the young lad". Photo: Henie Onstad archive.

→

First with the latest

As Sonja Henie's fame grew, she was asked more and more to promote sports, charity and other products. Photo: Henie Onstad archive.

→

The streaker

Sonja Henie's "signature" was a backwards glide ending with one leg high in the air. By the time she came to a stop on her tiptoe, her skirt had blown well over her back, to the crowd's great thrill. Photo: Henie Onstad archive.

←

Team captain

On 16 June 1928, the country's first public football match between two ladies' teams was held at Frogner Stadium. The proceeds went to the Order of Maria's charitable work. Sonja Henie captained the winning team. Photo: Henie Onstad archive.

←

St. Moritz, 1928

Sonja holding an exhibition in St. Moritz in connection with her very first Olympic gold. Photo: Henie Onstad archive.

↑

Icon

Sonja Henie is honoured in several public monuments. One is located between Kirkeveien and Frogner Stadium in Oslo. It was sculpted by Per Ung (1933–2013). As inspiration he used this picture of Sonja Henie in a classic pose from her victory on 5 February during the 1931 European championships in Vienna. The sculpture marks the entrance to the Sonja Henie ice rink. Photo: Henie Onstad archive.

→

St. Moritz, 1946

Henie trained to the very end. After giving up her status as an amateur, she used her skating skills in feature films and grand ice shows. Photo: Max Warner/ Henie Onstad archive.

←

Coach

St. Moritz, 1931. Handwritten on this picture: "The world's best coach, my good friend Brother Meyer". Photo: Henie Onstad archive.

↑

Well flanked

The 1931 European championships were held in Vienna and St. Moritz. Here, Sonja Henie is in Switzerland alongside world champion Karl Schäfer from Austria to her right and Swedish Olympic champion Gillis Grafström to her left. Photo: Henie Onstad archive.

←

Lake Placid, 9 February 1932

Sonja takes gold during the first Olympic figure skating to be held indoors. The programme was entitled "Ice Fairy". Photo: Abels Kunstforlag, Oslo/Henie Onstad archive.

→

Pavlova of the ice

Over a decade, Sonja changed figure skating. She helped popularise white skates and spectacular costumes. In addition, she made space for greater artistic latitude. This is from a show in Madison Square Garden, New York or the Palais des Sports in Paris, 1935. Photo: Henie Onstad archive.

Sonja Henie

↑

Advert for Norway

When Sonja Henie was invited to Madison Square Garden as a skating attraction on 6 January 1930, the plan was that the scenery would reproduce St. Moritz. It got the Norwegian press up in arms. Was Henie going to be advertising Switzerland? At the last moment, the title was changed to *In the Land of the Midnight Sun*. Upon her return to Oslo, she attended charity parades to benefit the sick and needy. Photo: Henie Onstad archive.

→

Skating, shows and film

In 1936, when Sonja Henie decided to end her amateur career and continue as a professional in showbiz and film, she moved to the United States. Flanked by the prize collection of a lifetime, and with new platinum blonde hair, a prom dress and a glittering smile, she brought together three different worlds. Photo: Henie Onstad archive.

↑

Party in Bislett

On 27 August 1938, Bislett Stadium was filled to the brim with 14,000 spectators to celebrate Sonja Henie. She was in Norway on the occasion of Norwegian premiere of her third film, *Happy Landing*. The party featured an extensive programme that included a singalong, tug of war and a beauty contest. Henie was driven up in a Horch car adorned with flowers, placed at her disposal by Berthel O. Steen. Photo: Henie Onstad archive.

THE BRAND

Sonja Henie was a superstar thirty years before the term was invented. She guaranteed sold-out cinemas and arenas – as long as she was working double.

Text: Gunhild Varvin

Sonja Henie used her name, media presence and skating talent to build a brand. She and the life she lived, were the product. As a pioneer, she had to figure things out on her own. There were no formulas or hard and fast rules. When she travelled to the United States in 1936, her background and star status were unmatched. Over several early trips and tours, she had been shown to be a big hit with audiences in North America. World-famous and used to winning, she started her life as a professional in the public eye. While today the creation and commercialising of distinctive identity on social media has become a career option for many, a hundred years ago this mentality was entirely novel. As such, Sonja Henie's innovation was the manipulation of a private life and a public persona into what would become a professional business career.

More work

After her fourth Olympics in 1936, Sonja Henie had decided to end her career in sport - but not to stop skating. Upon leaving Berlin she travelled to the European championships in St. Moritz and the world championships in Vienna. She won both. Then she arrived in Paris, held a grand exhibition to conclude her amateur career, and set sail from Le Havre. Together with her family and her skating partner Jack Dunn (1917–1938), she was ready for the United States. She had set her sights on a contract as a professional skater and film roles in the greatest dream factory of the age: Hollywood.

Stardom was nothing new to Sonja Henie. She had excelled with her figure skating shows ever since the 1920s. In addition to being an excellent athlete, she had learned to use her own persona to generate awareness of the sport and her performances. As a movie star in Hollywood, she would not have to work her way up through the ranks. She was aiming for the top from the get-go.

By the time Henie arrived in the United States in 1936, the star system had already been established. The major film studios used actors as a promotional focal point for their movies. In this way, they were brand names in predefined roles and genres. For example, the female actors had to fit roles as vamps or innocent beauties, or smaller supporting roles such as mothers, wives or teachers. Movies with child stars like Shirley Temple were a huge success. The roles guaranteed ticket sales and financing for future productions. Sonja Henie was already a character, but in Hollywood this was honed even further. She was given a more defined identity as an exclusive doll-woman from the north, with strong legs, blonde curls and blue eyes. She was positioned as an athletic hybrid in the form of a child star and an innocent beauty. The fact that she was actually dark blonde with brown eyes did not seem to matter much. In the film industry of the 1930s, fiction was reality.

Promoting Norway

From ever since Sonja Henie was a little girl, she had juggled entertainment, business, her star status and figure skating. She had learned to work double:

competing as an amateur and building her star status at the same time by providing entertainment to a paying audience. The historian Bodil Stenseth has written about how her father, Wilhelm Henie (1872–1937), was a behind-the-scenes negotiator and probably ensured the family's income from his daughter's performances.[1] She was allowed to advertise and generate income as long as it was for a charitable purpose. At the same time, she represented something greater: as an athlete, she was competing for Norway.

When Norwegian skaters travelled and made a name for themselves abroad, it stirred great excitement in Norway. However, there was also criticism that the Skating Federation and the Norwegian Olympic Committee spent too much money on the athletes' trips abroad. In response, the first "Festival of Fire" was held at Frogner Stadium in 1928. Sonja Henie agreed to appear as the main attraction, securing the organisers revenue of 16,000 kroner.[2]

The following year, at 17 years old, Henie – a deserving Norwegian, European, World and Olypmic champion – set out on her first major US tour. She agreed to perform as the main attraction in a show at Madison Square Garden, New York with the Viking age as a backdrop. The performance was for the benefit of orphaned children. The title would be A Night in St. Moritz. This triggered a storm of resentment in the Norwegian press. Would Sonja Henie be used to promote Switzerland?

"People are simply furious and a survey of [newspaper] *Nordisk Tidende*'s readers has led to a campaign against the organisers to get the framework and title changed in favour of Norway,"[3] wrote *Sportsmanden*, which was concerned that Henie's charity show ought to be promoting Norway. Pressure was put on the Norwegian sports authorities and on 12 November 1929, *Oslo Aftenavis* featured a caricature of the upcoming performance with Sonja Henie and her father Wilhelm on the ice alongside the text: "Sonja Henie advertises a Swiss sanatorium: 'Love it, just love it, thinking of daddy and moritz!'". After further impassioned protests, the title of the show was finally changed to *A Night in the Land of the Midnight Sun*. *Sportsmanden* provided regular updates and in the end was able to announce that the United States had fallen into line:

> "Since the huge commotion has been especially good publicity for our ice princess's performance here in New York and our campaign has given the Yankees the understanding that Norway is a country with as many attractions as sophisticated Switzerland, much has already been gained for Norwegian propaganda in the States and for our skating champion, whose performance is now also being welcomed with colossal interest by 100 per cent of Americans."

So it wasn't all about Sonja Henie; Norway's reputation and self-image was at stake, too.

Her performance in New York in 1930 was part of a larger US tour where Sonja Henie danced from city to city for packed arenas. The night out at Madison Square Garden was followed by performances at large ice rinks in a number of different states. The family were making new contacts and shows were selling out. With a choreography that included graceful ballet exercises, music and

[1] Stenseth, B, 2002: 91.
[2] Ibid s. 64.
[3] Sportsmanden, 1929.

dance, Sonja Henie's ice show drew comparisons to theatre and ice dance. The journey ended with a championship. On 3–5 February 1930, after many weeks of touring, Henie competed as a Norwegian athlete during the world championships in New York. As an athlete she had to be an amateur, that is, she was not allowed to sell tickets to her performances. It was only as a professional that she could earn good money. Sonja Henie dealt with this well and won the world championship in New York. Between the performances and the championship, she made good use of her time. Under the headline "Sonja's march of triumph", *Sportsmanden* reported:

> Sonja Henie has turned down a glittering film offer from Famous Players Lasky Corporation, which produces the famous Paramount Pictures. The reason for her refusal is that she also wishes to participate in the world championships in 1931 and the Winter Olympics in 1932... Had she accepted the offer to play in the film, she would undoubtedly have ice-skated in the film, and would thus become professional... Sonja does indeed want to act, but she has plenty of time and will be even more famous after 1932.[4]

Norwegians' pride in Sonja Henie seemed to be enormous – as long as she was promoting the right country.

Apolitical?

During their time as amateurs, Wilhelm and Sonja Henie repeatedly rejected rumours of lucrative activities which would have been in violation of applicable international rules. The accusations grew louder in connection with the Olympics in 1936, and this time it was not just Henie who would have to pay the price. Both the female and male favourites in figure skating, Sonja Henie from Oslo and Karl Schäfer (1909–1976) from Vienna, were accused of making money from illegal advertising activities. While Schäfer chose a strategy of keeping his mouth shut, Henie raised her head above the parapet and called a press conference. She denied rumours concerning her status as an amateur and announced some news that was much bigger than the accusations of commercial gain: The Olympics would be her very last competition. It was time to become professional.

There was an extraordinary backdrop to the 1936 Winter Olympics. Adolf Hitler (1889–1945) had come to power in Germany and the 1936 Olympic Games were being actively used as Nazi propaganda. The Führer and high-ranking officers watched from the stands. Hitler did not conceal his admiration for Sonja.[5] She had been a big star in the country for several years. With its large population, it was an important market for her, and her image and character were a good match for the Nazis' Aryan ideals. In Germany she had long gone by the nickname "Häschen", or Bunny, a name that was in circulation beyond the stands too; in his personal dedication on the portrait of himself that he presented to Henie in the 1930s, Hitler called her Bunny.

The first time Adolf Hitler met Sonja Henie was in connection with her

[4] *Sportsmanden*, 21 February 1930.
[5] Hambro, E. 1993.

performances at the Berlin Sportspalast in 1934. They then met two years later during Henie's competitive skating at the European championships in Berlin and perhaps during the Olympics in Garmisch-Partenkirchen a few weeks later in 1936.

The meeting during the European championships in 1936 was immortalised in a photograph that still circulates in the press and online. Henie performed at Berlin Sportspalast with Hitler, Goebbels and Göring in the stands. As she skated on the ice, she approached the Führer in the stands, then stopped to shake his hand. The picture shows Sonja Henie smiling coquettishly. We later learned that Hitler invited the entire Henie family to lunch, an offer they accepted. In his unauthorised biography following his sister's death, Henie's brother, Leif Henie, wrote that "The day after the performance, the Norwegian newspapers denounced Sonja in bold type: 'IS SONJA NAZI?' There was an outcry, not only in Norway, but all across Scandinavia."[6]

This writer has been unable to find any such clippings. On the contrary, the following year, in 1937, she was appointed a knight of St. Olav of the 1st class. At the ceremony, the mayor of Washington, D.C. handed her the key to the city, before the Norwegian ambassador, Wilhelm Morgenstierne, held a speech. He wished to "thank her on behalf of King Haakon for her efforts and for the healthy, sporty role model she has become for Norwegian youth".[7] She was the youngest ever recipient of such an award and the crowd that showed up to pay tribute was huge. She was more popular and beloved than ever before.

The meeting with Hitler, which may have seemed insignificant at the time, took on a new dimension after the war. It was then that the image of her shaking hands with Hitler began to circulate. If you Google "Sonja Henie" today, the articles linking the sports star with Nazism feature close to the top of the list. Following her death, the photograph has been revived time and time again. Most recently we saw how the image was brought up again when red, black and white ANTIFA stickers began to appear around Oslo in the spring of 2020.[8] In the wake of the Black Lives Matter movement, it was rightly pointed out how a number of public monuments have problematic backstories. The Sonja Henie statue at Frogner Stadium was included in a silent demonstration and was continuously pasted with new ANTIFA stickers over several months.

"Henie was used to rubbing shoulders with heads of state and royalty. What happened during the Olympics was more like a gesture of flattery, devoid of political significance", Henie biographer Mona Pedersen told NRK on the occasion of Sonja Henie's 100th birthday.[9] The sources confirm this. At the same time, Henie's meetings with Hitler show how not wanting to take an active political stance nevertheless ended up being interpreted in a political way. It also says something about the power of images and how stories that can be told more forcefully through photography than through words.

Hostility

The digital archives of the Associated Press show how, from January 1942, Sonja Henie made public her major financial contributions to the American forces.[10] She attended a range of charitable events and advertised cola drinks, among

[6] Henie, L. 2008:39.
[7] Hoel, M. L. 1992:36.
[8] ANTIFA står for antifascisme.
[9] https://www.nrk.no/sport/_-feil-a-lenke-henie-til-nazismen-1.8064886.
[10] http://www.apimages.com/.

other products, for the soldiers' benefit. At the same time, the biographies of Sonja Henie by Alf G. Andersen, Bodil Stenseth and Leif Henie reveal that when the war broke out in Norway, she was not ashamed of possessing a signed photograph of Hitler in her large collection of autographed portraits.[11] Instead of hiding it away, she made sure to place it on the grand piano at home in Landøya so everyone who entered the house could see it for themselves. When her films were refused German distribution in 1942, she called Minister of Propaganda Goebbels directly – and just like that, the matter was brought to a close. Despite her claims to the contrary, her actions were in fact political. Not taking a stance was a stance in itself.

In his biography, Alf G. Andersen refers to several sources which show that Henie donated money to the Norwegian forces during the war, albeit anonymously.[12] She also visited Norway several times after the war was over. But the visits were made in American uniform and received little press coverage. In her biography, Bodil Stenseth writes that if Sonja Henie's relationship with Norway was skewed, it was primarily because she did not visit the Norwegian Air Force in Canada until the winter of 1944.[13]

The various events during the war meant that while Sonja Henie's star rose to ever greater heights in the United States, the opposite happened in Norway. In her book about Henie, Merete Lie Hoel uses the Norwegian national character as an explanatory model. She points out that as a people, we "cannot abide anyone going beyond the norm".[14] Another explanation may be quite simply that after she became a US citizen, Henie no longer fulfilled Norway's desire for her to be a living ambassador for her homeland.

Photography

As soon as Sonja Henie made her entry into the United States in 1936, she turned professional in all meanings of the word. She was twenty-four years old. Photographs show how quickly Henie learned to find the camera. The blonde curls, the big, white smile, the short skirt and the sparkling blue eyes, which were actually brown.[15] Mass-produced images of her fit right into the Hollywood aesthetic of the 1930s and 1940s. As a forerunner to Marilyn Monroe and Esther Williams, and as a Nordic parallel to Ingrid Bergman in Hollywood, nothing was incidental. Her image would be built to perfection. Sonja Henie was one of the very first women in the world to carry out several training sessions daily. She was raised under a regime where grinding away at one's ambitions was the rule rather than the exception, and with her tremendous popularity she helped create a new ideal where women were active, participated in sports, competed and dared to pursue their goals.

The American film industry of the 1930s did not allow its stars to play roles that resembled their own lives too closely.[16] Henie broke with this rule. Henie's personal success was used as a natural backdrop for her new role as a movie star. Scripts for 20th Century Fox were written to parallel events in her own life, which is how she ended up playing characters mimicking the life she had lived as a skating star. Instead of building a new career as an actress, she would

[11] Sonja Henie collected signed portraits and received personal greetings from people such as Clark Gable, Adolf Hitler, Trygve Lie, Robert Kennedy and more.
[12] Andersen, A, 1985: 97.
[13] Stenseth, B, 2002: 194.
[14] Lie Hoel, M, 1992: 5.
[15] On the film posters, Sonja Henie's brown eyes were painted blue, in line with her Nordic brand identity.
[16] SCREEN, Sonja Henie's scrapbooks.

build on the star status she had already earned on the ice.

There are an overwhelming number of pictures of Sonja Henie. In the basement at Høvikodden are large piles of scrapbooks. Some she compiled herself, others were made by her many admirers. Even today, the art centre still receives cuttings and scrapbooks collected and assembled by fans all over the world. The books come in different shapes, some are made from wallpaper sample catalogues, others are sketchbooks or photo albums. It is touching to browse clippings accompanied by drawings and comments from fans. Many were made by young girls who followed their idol for years. We find tiny hearts and stars, carefully cut-out colour pictures taken from newspapers, magazines and weeklies. Some of the books were also made by the Henie family themselves. In them we find comments and remarks that reveal Sonja's willingness to shape her own brand. Both she and her parents have left notes on the back of photographs and next to the pasted clippings. Alongside a picture of Henie after two shows in Boston in 1937, for example, we can read her own comment that the red dress she wore does not photograph so well, a reminder for next time. The books can certainly be read as a sign of narcissism and self-obsession, but also as logbooks ensuring control over her own life and image. As such, Sonja Henie's active relationship to photography helped to define her as a brand and a person.

Target audience

Sonja Henie also had a very active relationship with her audiences. There were three occasions when great shifts occurred in her life. Each one was marked by the publication of a new autobiography. The books may not be interesting as works of literature, but when read as tools for repositioning a brand, there is much to be said for them.

My Life's Adventures was first released in 1938 with its target audience being Norwegians. The book revolved around Sonja Henie's transition from amateur figure skater to professional ice-skating and movie star in the United States. The text overlooked how she had abandoned Norway after her Olympic victory in 1936. Previously, she had always returned to Oslo after her big championship wins – and had been received like a queen. Instead of celebrating her victory with her countrymen, Henie had used the momentum provided by the gold medal to strike while the iron was hot in the United States.

The second autobiography had an American audience in mind. Entitled *Wings on My Feet*, it was published in the United States in 1940 and marked Sonja Henie's transition from maiden to married woman. No direct English translation of the Norwegian book from 1938 was published. This, rather, was a completely new autobiography, most of it rewritten. This time the background to the book was Henie's hit film *My Lucky Star*. The book was also given a completely new ending. With a manual and formula for how the readers themselves could learn to figure skate, the book had a new recurring theme with an even stronger central and commercial thrust: It's fun to go ice skating and you can actually try it yourself!

The target group for the third autobiography was once again Norwegians. The book was published in 1953 after Sonja Henie's huge performances at Jordal

Arena. After receiving little attention in Norway during the war, she had returned with a gigantic show. Now she was redefining herself again. Not only was she a skater and movie star, she was a first-class businesswoman and entertainer. Following her death, the book was reissued in 1977.

Surface and depth

In the American autobiography, Sonja Henie tells us that it was in the winter of 1934–35 that she realised that she had become a public figure.[17] She had barely reached the age of twenty when the press began in earnest to print stories about her love life, and she would stand smiling before the camera with the skater Jack Dunn, five years her junior. She commented that these kind of rumours were all part of the game for movie stars in Hollywood, but that it was embarrassing and unusual for a skating star.[18]

The pictures of her from those years demonstrate how she acted more and more professionally in front of the camera. At the same time as huge dramas were playing out in private, Henie's work rate picked up the pace. In 1937, not long after the Henie family had moved to the United States, Wilhelm Henie passed away. Sonja had just finished her first feature film, *One in a Million*. Family life and work life had gone hand in hand for as long as she could remember. Henie took her father's death hard, but did not stop making herself available for the press, her fans and her audience. She continued to build her lucrative brand. Then misfortune struck again. In late July of that year, Jack Dunn, her regular partner, died. They had made a joint decision to travel to the United States, they had stood side by side as they signed up as professionals, and they had both begun working as movie stars in Hollywood. Now that she was alone again, front-page stories circulated in the major international press about her romance with her next partner on the silver screen: Tyrone Power (1914–1958).

Amidst this chaos, she travelled back to Norway with her mother and brother. Her first feature film had already premiered in the major cities. During the last leg of her voyage from the United States, a large cortege of boats met her on the Oslo Fjord. They were there to escort Norway's first, major movie star safely back onto the Oslo quayside.

She had lost her father and her closest partner, and had committed to starring in two feature films a year while touring across the United States with what would become a very famous show on ice. Just as she did everything she could to avoid falling on the ice, her public appearances were the epitome of assured self-control. In the photo archives, there is no hint of grief. Henie continued to smile as she stubbornly carried on working. Her tireless will and ability to keep going was a strategy she held on to for the rest of her life, even as she set out to build an art collection. As she said at the time, "I need to see the future ahead of me, not just look backwards".[19]

[17] Henie, S. 1940: 67.
[18] Ibid
[19] Hoel, M. L. 1992.

Dual business concept

Henie had barely attended school and had only just turned twenty years old when hard-working businessmen such as Arthur M. Wirtz (1901–1983) of Wirtz Corporation and Darryl Zanuck (1902–1979) from Twentieth Century Pictures (later Fox) entered her life. They would become powerful partners within showbusiness in the United States. Wirtz did his first deal with Henie and her father as far back as 1935 when they put on a figure skating show for two nights in Chicago.

The following year, they signed a permanent contract. This gave Henie top billing. He held an effective monopoly over skating rinks across large swathes of the country, and she would fill them. Zanuck, one of Hollywood's leading producers, signed a contract with Henie in 1936 after seeing her perform in a well-directed ice show over two nights in LA. The contract secured Twentieth Century a long line of blockbusters. Sonja Henie was the hot ticket in what would become a new genre in Hollywood: the skating movie. Sonja Henie played characters largely modelled on her own persona, her own exploits on skates, and the speculation about her that circulated in the press. Fact and fiction, public and private, was all stirred together in a cheerful blend which had massive public appeal during the Depression of the 1930s. Both Wirtz and Zanuck were cut-throat businessmen. Because he worked around the clock, Wirtz's initials, A. M., were said to stand for "after midnight".[20] Zanuck, for his part, broke with Warner Bros. to develop their rival Twentieth Century Fox, with great success.[21] But Sonja Henie courted them both. By creating synergies between the two giants in their respective fields, she built up her own enterprise.

She took chances and created opportunities instead of waiting for them to come her way. While Wirtz and Zanuck each made lucrative deals with Henie, she operated a dual business concept. By alternating between starring in Zanuck's major Hollywood films and collaborating with Wirtz to put on massive touring ice shows, she attracted hordes of spectators. Wirtz and Henie's production in New York, It Happens on Ice, sold 1.5 million tickets in 1940 alone. She – the brand Sonja Henie – was central to the strategy, carefully patented and commercialised in the form of clothing, paper dolls, Christmas tree decorations, on posters advertising everything from washing powder to homestyle chicken – and books. The person who looked after these sidelines and the Sonja Henie trademark was her brother, Leif Henie. As the one in charge of the family's fur boutique in Oslo, it was he who started producing clothing collections based on outfits worn by Sonja's movie characters. He sold them exclusively from the store on Prinsens gate in Oslo. Soon, paper dolls and sketchbooks joined the ranks of souvenirs and collectibles. Finally, in 1953, he was also listed as "Vice President and Treasurer" for Sonja Henie Ice Revue – although the company bore her name, and she was ultimately the boss.

[20] http://www.fundinguniverse.com/company-histories/wirtz-corporation-history/.
[21] https://www.britannica.com/biography/Darryl-F-Zanuck.
[22] Hoel, M. L. 1992:65.

From Hollywood to Høvikodden

After two marriages to Americans – Dan Topping (1912–1974) in 1940 and Winthrop Gardiner (1912–1980) in 1949 – Sonja Henie married for a third time in 1956. In the summer of 1955, she met the Norwegian Niels Onstad while she was in Norway. They married the following year in New York. She had put a lot of energy into becoming American and laughed when she met the press: "I fooled you all. None of you guessed that I would marry a Norwegian!"[22]

Meeting Niels Onstad marked a new turning point in her life. He had long had a genuine interest in contemporary art, something that initially irritated her. *Aftenposten* reported her reaction in 1960:

"If I'm going to move in here then you can get rid of this rubbish," she said generously to her new husband of his collection.

"But then, little by little, she started buying modern paintings first, and then other things. Now she cannot talk for five minutes without talking about paintings. She runs up and down the stairs, lively as a squirrel, to retrieve catalogues from this auction or brochures from that collection, she knows at a glance where such and such image is in so and so collection in Zurich, Paris or New York, and she has the same zeal when it comes to getting to grips with it all as she would were it a new Olympic championship", wrote Aftenposten when Sonja Henie and Niels Onstad's plans for a new museum at Høvikodden were announced.[23]

Eight years later, in connection with the building's opening, the couple was interviewed and asked about the centre's financial prospects:

"'I envisage the possibility that it can be self-sustaining,' Onstad claimed. It is obvious that he is not prepared simply to play the role of Santa Claus at Høvikodden. Through Sonja's brown-eyed gaze, however, runs a distinct ripple of scepticism. It is clear that the showbusiness expert sees no glimpses of financial success with this project. 'The general public are not so interested in art,' she says."[24]

What remains

In the bookshelves of the archive at Høvikodden, we find pictures that show Sonja Henie over a lifetime. But despite the abundance of images, there are few official texts in Henie's own hand in the rich archive of documents. It is Niels Onstad's typewritten words we find, and it is his name that heads the list of speakers at the opening. In writing, we find only a few simple remarks about Sonja Henie introducing King Olav V's speech at the art centre. Were it not for her personal letters, her countless interviews, press clippings and photos that show her as the focal point she undoubtedly was, we would hardly have known she was there.

There is a great gulf between the centre's written and visual archives. While she dominates the press clippings section, she is scarcely present in the official documents. Is this do with Sonja Henie's own style – or the expectations after which she must, to a certain extent, have styled herself?

In any case, one thing is certain. Sonja Henie made sure to credit the people she teamed up with. One example is how she underscored that her holiday

[23] *Aftenposten* 8.11.1960.
[24] *Morgenbladet* 13.08.1968.
[25] Henie S. 1953.

spot on Landøya was first and foremost a place for her father.[25] Another is how, in working towards the art centre at Høvikodden, she explained that between the two of them, Niels Onstad was the experienced art collector. Without him, the idea of the museum would likely not have seen the light of day. Nevertheless, it is Sonja Henie's name that was given to the two roads that lead to Landøya and Høvikodden. Neither is a main thoroughfare. They are, rather, short sideroads with limited views, scattered buildings, a lot of weeds and many trees.

Conflict

Stories about Sonja Henie reveal an interesting interplay between the distinctiveness of the brand she created and the conflicts that still breathe fresh life into the narrative around it. The more innocent, polished and professional Sonja Henie appeared as a brand, the stronger the contrast would seem if she could be associated with the opposite. All good stories contain this tension. It revolves around novelty, relevance and contrast. Henie's rich life and spectacular persona can still create headlines. The sheer magnitude of it all gives it power.

As such, Sonja Henie's legacy in Norway is characterised by a duality: Idol worship of an extremely talented athlete and beautiful film actress on the one hand; jealousy, opportunism and flirtations with Nazism on the other. With her lavish lifestyle and of three marriages, Henie starred in a drama the likes of which Norway had never before seen. She claimed a position for herself no one else before her had taken.

Sources:

Andersen, Alf G., *Som i en drøm. Sonja Henies liv*, Oslo, 1985

Berg, Anne Kari, *Heltinner. Kvinnelige ikoner i det 20. århundre*, Spartacus, Oslo, 1998

Finborud, Lars Mørch, *Mot det totale museum*, Press, 2012

Hambro, Edvard, *Isens dronning*, NRK, 1993

Henie, Sonja, *Mitt livs eventyr*, Gyldendal Norsk Forlag, 1938

Henie, Sonja, *Wings on My Feet*, Hurst & Blackett Ltd., 1940

Henie, Sonja, *Mitt livs eventyr*, Gyldendal Norsk Forlag, 1953

Hoel, Merete Lie, *Sonja Henie*, Oslo, 1992

Pedersen, Mona, *Henie i Hollywood, Norsk filminstitutts skriftserie*, 16, 2002

Stenseth, Bodil, *Sonja Henie, Kvinne på is*, Pax Forlag A/S, Oslo, 2002

Strait, Raymond, Henie, Leif, *Min søster Sonja Henie. I sin egen skygge*, Juritzen forlag, 2008

Moe, Ole Henrik, *Sonja Henies bilder- malerier og fotografier 1969-1970*, Henie Onstad Kunstsenter, 1969

Jacobs, Laura, Sonja Henie's Ice Age, Vanity Fair, 11. februar 2014: https://www.vanityfair.com/hollywood/2014/02/sonja-henie-ice-skating-queen

The personal clipping archive from Sonja Henie

Archives of documents, press and letters, Henie Onstad Kunstsenter, 1920-1969.

NTB, AP, Getty og Alamy image archives.

Blogs:

http://skateguard1.blogspot.com/2020/06/the-1936-european-figure-skating.html?m=1

Oral sources:

Ole Henrik Moe (1920–2013)

Reidar Børjeson (1931–2011)

FILMOGRAFI (Filmography)

1927, Syv dage for Elisabeth, Norge.

1929, Se Norge, (dokumentar), Norge.

1936, Isens dronning (One in a Million), USA, Twentieth Century-Fox Film Corporation.

1937, På glattisen (Thin Ice), USA, Twentieth Century-Fox Film Corporation.

1937, Ali Baba (Ali Baba Goes to Town), USA, Twentieth Century-Fox Film Corporation.

1938, Happy Landing, USA, Twentieth Century-Fox Film Corporation.

1938, En mannequin på college (My Lucky Star), USA, Twentieth Century-Fox Film Corporation.

1939, Annen fiolin (Second Fiddle), USA, Twentieth Century-Fox Film Corporation.

1939, Til Vesterheimen, Norge, Oslo Kinematografer (oppdragsgiver).

1939, Journalist på eventyr (Everything Happens at Night), USA, Twentieth Century-Fox Film Corporation.

1941, Høyfjellets sang (Sun Valley Serenade), USA, Twentieth Century-Fox Film.

1942, Iceland, USA, Twentieth Century-Fox Film.

1943, Wintertime, USA, Twentieth Century-Fox Film.

1945, Amor på glattisen (It's a Pleasure), USA, International Pictures, Inc.

1948, Grevinnen av Monte Cristo (The Countess of Monte Cristo), USA, Westwood Corporation.

1960, Hallo London (Hello London), Storbritannia, Eastmancolor.

↑

The decision

Sonja Henie and the British figure skater Jack Dunn met in St. Moritz in 1934. They became a couple and they took a joint decision to become professional skaters. Dunn died in the United States only two years later on 16 July 1938. From left: Selma Henie, Sonja Henie and Jack Dunn. Photo: Henie Onstad archive.

→

New career

All of Sonja Henie's Hollywood scripts for 20th Century Fox were written to resemble events in her own life. That's how she ended up playing characters mimicking the life she had lived as a skating star. Instead of building a new career as an actress, she was able to build on the star status she had already earned on the ice rink. Photo: 20th Century Fox/Henie Onstad archive.

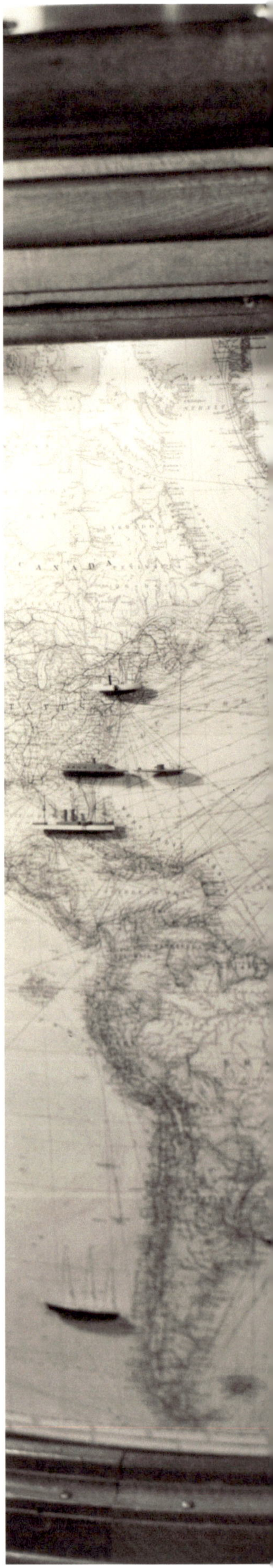

RAND McNALLY · INTERNATIONAL EDITION
WORLD ATLAS
WORLD ATLAS

←

Headliner in St. Moritz

Henie's name had had top billing for several years before she turned professional. Here she towers above the Canada All Stars and the American film comic Harold Lloyd, who was as big as Charlie Chaplin and Buster Keaton in his time. Photo: Henie Onstad archive.

→

White swan

Sonja Henie brought much novelty to the male-dominated world of skating. With distinctive outfits, elegance, the will to win and sheer muscle power, she exemplified a more active female ideal. Instead of contenting herself with cheering on the boys, she secured herself a place at the heart of the action. Photo: Henie Onstad archive.

←

Front-page material

Sonja Henie was in the public eye from when she won the figure skating championship at the age of nine. In the press, her life was in the public domain – this was before the framework for the media ethics were enshrined in official documents. The many press rumours about her amateur status contributed to her decision to move to the United States in 1936. Photo: Henie Onstad archive.

EDMONTON

←

PR

When Sonja Henie turned professional, a carefully programmed skating show was held over two days in Hollywood. The goal was to land a good film contract. Many members of the film industry were there and she made a splash. The address of Hollywood agent Charles Beyer is noted on her private programme. Beyer was associated with the 20th Century Fox production company. Photo: Henie Onstad archive.

↓

20th Century Fox, 1936

With her mother Selma Henie behind her, Sonja Henie negotiated a lucrative film contract with Daryl Zanuck at 20th Century Fox. He offered her skating parts in his films. Henie turned him down: she wanted the lead roles as well. And that's what she got. Filming for Henie's first film, *One in a Million*, began in September of that year. Photo: Henie Onstad archive.

→

Behind the scenes

Until his death in 1937, Wilhelm Henie was credited as the family strategist. He often appeared in the press, spoke on Sonja Henie's behalf and secured useful contacts and business connections. Photo: Henie Onstad archive.

→

Her own image

Sonja in the dressing room for a show in Boston, 1937. On the back of the picture she has noted that the red dress did not photograph very well. By evaluating her own performances, she gave herself greater and greater definition as a brand. Photo: Henie Onstad archive.

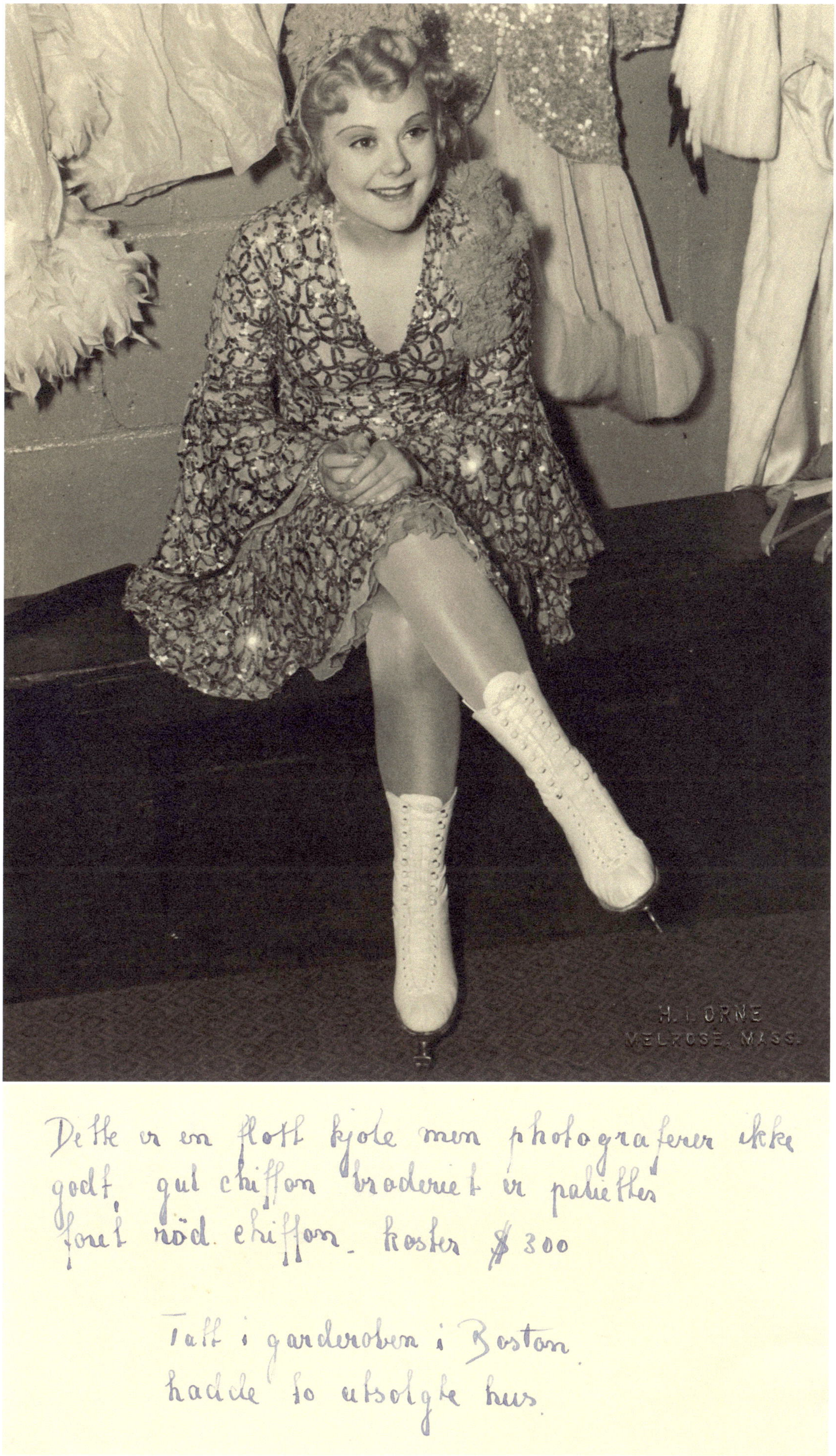

←

25-year-old knight

In gratitude for the healthy, sporty role model she had become for Norwegian youth, in December 1937 Sonja Henie was appointed a Knight of St. Olav of the first class during a grand reception in Washington. Photo: Washington Herald Staff Photo/Henie Onstad archive.

↑

Oslo, 1937

In August, shortly after the deaths of two vital men, her father Wilhelm Henie and partner Jack Dunn, Sonja Henie arrived in Oslo by sea. Her reception as a movie star surpassed anything she had previously experienced as a skating star. A huge cortege of boats accompanied her to the VIP quay in Oslo. Photo: Henie Onstad archive.

→

Mourning in the public eye

Sonja Henie did not shy away from her duties. In a black mourning veil, she greeted the public among a sea of flowers. Her mother Selma persevered – right behind her daughter. The wild enthusiasm on Henie's homecoming was compared to the reception of Amundsen on his return from the South Pole. Photo: Henie Onstad archive.

→

My Lucky Star, 1938

After barely two years in the film industry, Sonja Henie was preparing for her fourth major film premiere. She starred opposite Richard Greene in *My Lucky Star*. Photo: Henie Onstad archive.

←

The dream factory

After her father and partner Dunn passed away, romantic rumours surrounding Sonja Henie's private life were always in the news. There was much speculation about her relationship with actor Tyrone Power. To maximise the news value of the films she starred in, several of the love stories were pure spin – and often directed by the film company she was working for. Photo: Henie Onstad archive.

←

Newly blonde

In Hollywood, the skating star was transformed into a superstar. Everything from her clothing, hairstyle and public statements became part of the act. The Sonja Henie brand acquired an American identity. Photo: Henie Onstad archive.

BANNER
MILK

↑

Grauman Theatre, 1937

After *Thin Ice*, her second feature film, the blades of Henie's ice skates were cast in concrete outside the Grauman Chinese Theater along with her greeting: TIL LYKKE ALWAYS. It's still there to this very day, alongside the imprints of Fred Astaire, Ginger Rogers, Tyrone Power, Shirley Temple and others. Photo: Henie Onstad archive.

→

Golden Age

The 1930s were a time of depression and Hollywood created dreams based on the classic movie formula. With glamour, joy and a high "wow" factor on skates, Sonja Henie was a good fit for the musical segment. Based on her appearance as a child star, Henie's films defined skating films as a new category. Great emphasis was placed on extravagant costumes, beautiful scenery, strong showmanship and simple romantic plots without too much dialogue. Here is Sonja Henie with Shirley Temple. Photo: 20th Century Fox/Henie Onstad archive.

←

Athlete

She was the product, her achievements on the ice and her vow that she would always win. With her body in focus, Sonja Henie pushed back many boundaries. Photo series from Berlin, 1936. Photo: Henie Onstad archive.

→

Her own image

"She had style, artistic skills and was an athlete, but most importantly for that period was that she had guts. She dared to pursue her own ideas – she chased the image she had of herself," said Peggy Fleming, 1968 Olympic figure skating gold medallist, to *Vanity Fair* regarding Sonja Henie. Photo: Henie Onstad archive.

↑

Chicago, 1938

When she was done competing as an athlete, she redefined herself. In her new life in America, the ice became an important ingredient in major Hollywood productions, shows and advertising stunts. Following two test shows with the impresario Arthur Wirtz in Chicago back in 1935, the two of them signed a long-term contract when she turned professional. Since Wirtz controlled a large proportion of the skating rinks in the United States and Henie was a permanent fixture in leading roles for the film giant 20th Century Fox, their partnership gathered huge crowds for her shows. Photo: Henie Onstad archive.

SONJA HENIE WITH HER
HOLLYWOOD ICE REVUE
PRESENTED BY
CHICAGO STADIUM CORP.
DEC. 25TH TO 31ST 1938

↑

One in a Million, 1936

The shows were extravagant and just the prop rig for Sonja Henie's very first film, *One in a Million*, was enormous. The plot was set in St. Moritz in Switzerland and she played the character Greta Müller, with a script that resembled Sonja's own life very closely. The Swiss backdrop stirred Norway's desire to be part of Henie's success and it was bitterly remarked that the setting ought to have been Norwegian. Photo: *One in a Million*, 1936, 20th Century Fox/Henie Onstad archive.

Dette er Valsen
dette er taget under
prøve, Sonja er ikke
på billedet men hun
danser i midten

Det er ordentlige
trær som er
sprøitet maling
på, ser ut som
pine

Dette er skøitebanen
hos Fox.

Den sorte bakgrund
blir malt fjelder i St. Moritz
og måskin, det blir sat til
efter på

286P/21

Last minute instructions are given the ice-skating chorus of 42 girls in the musical extravaganza, "One In A Million", a Sonja Henie starring vehicle at 20th Century-Fox, before the scene is filmed. Jack Haskell, dance director, may be seen silhouetted in foreground in topcoat and hat, talking to Kenny Williams, assistant dance director, in sweater in spotlight.

H/S
392
S.H.

↑

On the reverse

It is not only Sonja Henie's personal notes that accompany images in the Henie Onstad archive. Her parents' texts also feature: "This is the 'waltz'. This was taken during rehearsal, Sonja is not in the picture, but she is dancing in the middle. Those are real trees that have been spray-painted to look like pine. Mountains and moonshine in St. Moritz will be painted on the black background afterwards." The whole family paid close attention during the shooting of her first movie. Photo: Henie Onstad archive.

←

Starring Sonja Henie

By continually playing herself, it became difficult to see the differences between private and public life, the real and the imagined. With her figure skater's iron will, Henie was very preoccupied with the music and the visual quality of her films. If there was something she didn't like, she said so. Photo: Henie Onstad archive.

→

Black Ice

"I want to do with skates what Fred Astaire is doing with dancing," Henie said when she retired as a competitive athlete in 1936. With an eye for detail, she helped develop black ice. A blue-black liquid was poured over the ice's surface so that her mirror image was reflected in the ice. Photo: From *Wintertime*, 1943/ 20th Century Fox/Henie Onstad archive.

→

Colours

Hand-painted photographs marketed her films both in the press and in larger advertising campaigns. Sonja Henie was constantly presented more and more like a doll, in short skirt and white skates that were sold in her name to an ever growing audience. Photo: *My Lucky Star*, 1938/20th Century Fox/Henie Onstad archive.

←

Black & white

It wasn't long after Henie made her Hollywood debut that she was a top-earning actress. She was a good fit for the studios' star system, where they had stables of actors to fill various roles and functions. Sonja Henie was perfect as an innocent child-woman and also had an exotic streak – she represented Europe and could dance on ice. Photo: *My Lucky Star*, 1938/ 20th Century Fox/Henie Onstad archive.

↑

Chesterfield

After eight years in Hollywood, Henie broke away from her image as an innocent, sporty, child-woman. She appeared in advertisements for cigarettes and increasingly played on an image of sexy seductiveness. But she didn't drop the skates. They were with her all her life. Facsimile: Henie Onstad archive.

←

New star

Allowing Henie to promote canaries fit perfectly with the target group 20th Century Fox had in mind for her. With her massive appeal to children, young women and families with children, a big push was made for her to promote the right products. Facsimile: Henie Onstad archive.

↑

Milk

Ever since she was a little girl, Sonja Henie had appeared in promotions for Norwegian products and services. After arriving in the USA, ads for Wilhelm Henie's fur store in Oslo and public awareness campaigns for milk were replaced by giants such as Coca-Cola and Chesterfield. Facsimile: Henie Onstad archive.

↑

My Life's Adventures

Sonja Henie launched her first autobiography in 1938 to mark her transition from skater to movie star. Photo: Henie Onstad archive.

→

Prinsens gate 12

Her father Wilhelm Henie's fur store in Oslo was used as an office to schedule Sonja Henie tours and as the setting for interviews, and was the place where her costumes were planned and later copied and sold. Photo: Henie Onstad archive.

↑

Persil

In many ways, since the 1920s Sonja had anticipated the Hollywood star system in which the actors were used as a natural promotional focus. The only difference was that Henie as a skater was not acting in a movie; she used her own life to live as the character of Sonja Henie. Here she provides the setting for Persil detergent. Facsimile: Henie Onstad archive.

→

Exclusive rights

In addition to performing, Sonja Henie used her name along with external partners, to sell everything from washing powder, chicken and cigarettes to fur from her father's business. Her brother Leif Henie patented his sister's outfits in her popular films. Photo: Henie Onstad archive.

←

The making of a star

In the 1930s, studios had their own methods for making a movie star. Training was given in diction, song, dance, language and sport. It was quite normal to have cosmetic surgery and change one's name. Sonja Henie was cultivated as a little doll. Facsimile: Henie Onstad archive.

→

The cake decoration

Sonja Henie's image was honed throughout her appearances in big ice shows. Despite the fact that she herself was growing older, she did not allow her persona to do so. It was perfectly natural, then, that she should occupy the top of a cake in outfits whose hems never ceased to creep higher and higher. Photo: Henie Onstad archive.

↑

Spin off

Sonja Henie's story was often told as a doll story with children as the target group. The medium was colouring books which dealt with her background in Norway, the fact that she enjoyed skiing, and that she had a brother. All of this was told though drawings depicting her as an innocent little girl in a child's bedroom. Facsimile: Henie Onstad

→

Blue-eyed

Unlike most other newcomers to Hollywood, Sonja Henie did not have to work her way up through the star system. She burst right into number eight on the box office charts and earned $500,000 in her first year. After a fresh round of negotiations, for a time she was the highest paid star in Hollywood. Through simple retouching, the brown-eyed woman was given the bluest eyes in Hollywood. Facsimile: Henie Onstad archive.

←

The imagined Bunad

In the United States, Henie could present Europe as an exotic destination. Her costumes were designed like a potpourri, with ingredients from the Norwegian national dress "bunad", German Tyrolean outfits, and Swiss patterning. Photo: 20th Century Fox/Henie Onstad archive.

→

Superstar

Sonja Henie was a superstar three decades before the term was coined by Andy Warhol in the 1960s. In Hollywood, her nose was operated on, her eyebrows were narrowed, her hair was bleached and her eyelashes became as long and as false as Marlene Dietrich's. Photo: 20th Century Fox/Henie Onstad archive.

↓

In person

Henie Onstad Kunstsenter's cuttings archive contains Sonja Henie's personal scrapbooks, with shelves of press coverage, advertisements and photos. Here she is often presented "as herself" in photographs and colourised press cuttings. Facsimile: Henie Onstad archive.

←

Pro

The difference between depth and surface, real and paid-for is something we are increasingly aware of. Today, official rules and guidelines exist for product placement and sponsorship agreements. When Sonja Henie drew up her business concept, she had to beat her own path. She usually chose the most lucrative option. Photo: Henie Onstad archive.

↑

Car

Sonja Henie was not just a skater and a movie star, she was also a brand and a businesswoman like no one else before her.
In Hollywood, she attracted plenty of attention in her cream-white car with a red leather finish.
To complement it all she would usually wear white outfits. Photo: Henie Onstad archive.

→

At home with

In familiar "at home with" style, the colour press provided intricate stories about Sonja's private life, recipes and fashion tips, everything richly illustrated with the lead character herself, posing in gorgeous outfits – often with references to where they could be purchased. Photo: Henie Onstad archive.

TO SONJA

To Sonja

For Sonja
With love
Lucy

To Sonja —
All best wishes

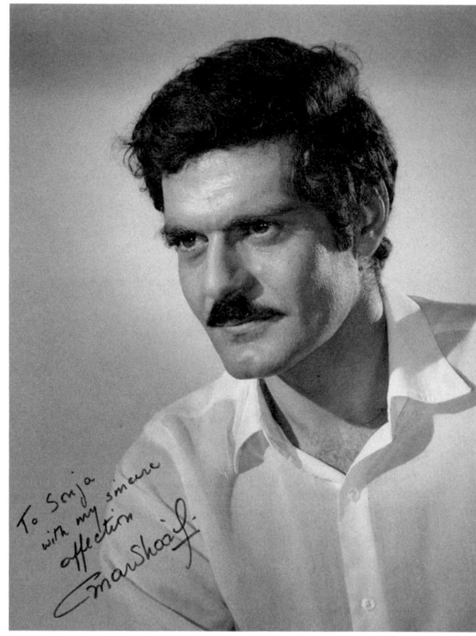
To Sonja
with my sincere
affection

For Sonja Henie
With best wishes

Till kära Sonja, med hälsning från oss alla
1959

Kindest regards to
Mr. + Mrs. Nick Onstad
1/4/64

To Sonja –
With love and
admiration,
Natalie

1/3/64

To
Sonja
Always
Dean Martin

To Sonja Henie
My best wishes
Walt Disney

To Sonja from one fan
to another! – Ingrid

To Sonja + Niels –
With all good wishes!
Julie Andrews
JA-17

For Sonja –
from he who skates on
thinner ice!
Cary

To Sonja Henie
love
Shirley Temple.

Dear Sonja -
All the best -
Good luck -
Gene Kelly

To
SKATEY
with love

To Sonja Henie
With most cordial regards
J Edgar Hoover
3.22.65

Kjære Sonja og Niels.
Med hilsen fra
Deres
Trygve
24/2.1964

With best wishes,
Jacqueline Kennedy

←

Skis and knitted mittens

Norway was added as an exotic ingredient to Henie's American films. Garments inspired by national dress, cardigans and the classic knitted mittens helped to symbolise something new, European and different. Photo: Henie Onstad archive.

→

The winter experience

Skating and skiing became fashionable and part of a new trend in which taking part in winter sporting activities grew in popularity. The scenes in Henie's films served as inspiration and she promoted them with lessons in skating and skiing techniques. Photo: Henie Onstad archive.

↑

Thin Ice

It is almost 100 years since Sonja Henie started to explore issues around how content and ideas could be spread organically or through sponsorship. She was also ground-breaking in terms of her use of product placement. Like a present-day reality star, she played herself in eleven major silver-screen Hollywood productions. Each film was marketed like the great American dream. Photo: Henie Onstad archive.

↑

Hitler

During the 1936 European championships in Berlin, Sonja Henie shook hands with Adolf Hitler, standing with Hans von Tschammer, Osten and Joseph Goebbels (far right). Three years before war broke out, the competition was heavily marked by German Nazi propaganda. The act was likely motivated by an opportunistic desire to win the championship. Today, the question of whether she was a Nazi still clings to her legacy. "Nazi schmazi, I don't even know what Nazism is," she is reported to have said. It is difficult to say whether she understood the political scope of her gesture. Photo: Schirner Sportfoto/AP Images/Henie Onstad archive.

←

Royal Crown Cola

Like many American film stars, Henie actively collected money for the allied forces during the war. In this ad she promoted the sale of war bonds at the same time as advertising Royal Crown Cola and her own film *It's a Pleasure* from 1945. Facsimile: Henie Onstad archive.

→

Allied supporter

Press clip showing that in 1942 (perhaps even earlier), Sonja Henie made an active public effort to distance herself from the German superpower. She donated anonymously to the Norwegian resistance and participated in shows and press stunts. Here she is travelling in a plane with paratroopers. She has written "I dont whant to jump" in neat handwriting. She received a parachuting certificate, nonetheless. Photo: Henie Onstad archive.

d dont want to jum
Col.

←

Premiere party

Rumours abounded about Sonja Henie's extraordinary annual garden parties on Delfern Drive in Hollywood. She is said to have had live swans in the pool, huge flower arrangements, elephants on the lawn and all the right guests. Photo: Henie Onstad archive.

↑

First colour movie

It's a Pleasure from 1945 was Sonja Henie's first film in Technicolor. Although the plot was thin, the skating scenes were extraordinary. Facsimile: Henie Onstad archive.

←

Clark Gable

Married couple Clark and Kay Gable were two of Sonja Henie's close friends and neighbours in Hollywood. In private Clark is said to have strummed a guitar while Sonja danced. Photo: Henie Onstad archive.

→

Full control

From being an athlete who competed with the Norwegian flag on her chest and always won, Henie repositioned her identity towards being American. In 1945, she was no longer the young sports heroine who travelled the world to bring Norwegian victories home. She was a superstar with American citizenship, a circle of celebrity friends, and spectacular LA garden parties. Photo: Henie Onstad archive.

←

The perfect hostess

Sonja Henie was good at mingling from group to group at her parties and wanted to be sure everyone was having a good time. She checked her guest lists closely and kicked out anyone who failed to follow protocol or drank too much. Photo: Henie Onstad archive.

←

Alfred Hithcock and Ingrid Bergman

In the 1930s and 1940s, the Hollywood movie scene was intimate and marked by a family of stars where "everyone knew everyone". As a matter of course, all the big stars attended each other's parties. Photo: Henie Onstad archive.

↑

Personal and private

Sonja Henie was often photographed in very intimate settings, like here, right inside her own bedroom. This type of image reveals the gulf we see between the written and visual archives that Henie Onstad Kunstsenter has inherited. While Sonja Henie dominates the press clippings and private photo department, she is almost absent in the official documents. Is this a result of her own style – or the expectations based on which she must, to a certain extent, have styled herself? Photo: Henie Onstad archive.

→

Hollywood Ice Revue

Effectively marketed through the image of the easily recognisable doll-woman on skates, Sonja Henie was always creating momentum. She alternated between playing the lead role on skates in major Hollywood movies and putting on massive touring ice shows. She attracted enormous audiences. In 1940 alone, the New York production *It Happens on Ice* sold 1.5 million tickets. Facsimile: Henie Onstad archive.

Sonja Henie
Hollywood Ice Revue

↑

Marriage #1

She became a US citizen in 1940 when she got married for the first time, to Dan Topping (1912–1974).

↗

Marriage #2

After the breakdown of her marriage during the war, she got married again, to Winthrop "Winnie" Gardiner (1912–1980).

→

Marriage #3

In 1956 she got married for the third and final time to the Norwegian Niels Onstad (1909–1978). The marriage resulted in Henie Onstad Kunstsenter in Bærum, outside Oslo. She donated the fortune she had built up over a lifetime in the spotlight to create and run the centre. Photo: Henie Onstad archive.

←

Lion

After the plans to create a huge museum for contemporary art took shape as the 1950s turned into the 1960s, Sonja Henie spent more and more time in Norway. But she never relinquished her American identity. Here she is at a restaurant with her husband Niels Onstad (outside the frame) and an unknown lion cub in the 1960s. Photo: Henie Onstad archive.

→

Jordal Arena, 1953.

Despite the fact that Sonja Henie had visited Norway many times after the war, it wasn't until 1953 in connection with her big show at Jordal Arena in Oslo that she was hailed in the style to which she was accustomed before the outbreak of war. Facsimile: Henie Onstad archive.

←

Hestnes

Norwegian journalists were welcome to Sonja Henie's home on Delfern Drive. Here is *Dagbladet*'s reporter Arne Hestnes getting a private tour of the property. In the background is the sculpture *Esprit, Eau et Sang* (1961) by Émile Gilioli. Today it is part of the sculpture park around Henie Onstad Kunstsenter in Høvikodden. Photo: Henie Onstad archive.

CUBA

When her career was on the decline, Sonja Henie found new inspiration in Havana – and reconquered Oslo.

Text: Martine Hoff Jensen

In Cuba in 1952, Sonja was seduced – by dance. Henie had earlier impressed her audience with the Hawaiian number *Fantasy from Hawaii*. At a Cuban nightclub, she was introduced to rhythms and body movements that ignited a fire in her, and the result was a new "fire dance" for her repertoire on the ice. With her from Havana she took the two dancers who had inspired her, Marta and Alexander.

A flair for trends

Sonja Henie was early to catch on to new trends. As far back as 1953, she wanted to create a three-dimensional skating movie.[1] When she later began collecting art, she preferred innovative and abstract works that captured the spirit of the times. However, it was through her skating shows that we were first introduced to Sonja Henie as a selling machine. It was here that she revealed her gift for business. The exoticism of the period was presented as a novelty to the ice rink – and it was a hit.

By 1952, a financial slump that began two years earlier forced Henie to think afresh. Her second husband, Winthrop "Winnie" Gardiner, had persuaded Sonja to part ways with her business partner of thirteen years, Arthur M. Wirtz. Winnie thought that she should run the ice shows alone so that she wouldn't have to share her earnings. This, however, led to financial disaster. Wirtz's background was as a broker in the real-estate business and he had started buying up large arenas in the 1930s. By the 1950s, he controlled every sports arena east of the Mississippi. When Henie abruptly ended their partnership, for him it was simply a question of setting up his own tour with Barbara Ann Scott, Henie's rival on the ice. Henie had to be content with smaller arenas.[2] Even when garnering good reviews and attracting strong audiences, the limited capacity of the ice stadiums resulted in the shows not generating enough income. She also had to book all the shows herself, buy equipment and costumes, and hire and pay up to two hundred people, all of whom she travelled with around the United States on her own train. It quickly became a drain on the budget instead of the licence to print money she – or rather Winnie – had imagined.

Rhythms to the fore

After a disappointing US tour, Henie decided to perform a series of shows in Cuba. In Havana, her ice revue was adapted to the theatre stage at Teatro Blanquita, a venue that was both available and met Henie's requirements for size and seating capacity.[3] During her stay in the Cuban capital, Henie visited the Sans Soucí nightclub in Arroya Arena, located about 15 kilometres outside the city, with some members of the ensemble. The Caribbean rhythms were to her liking and she immediately decided to adapt the dances for skates. Henie invited the dancers from the nightclub, Marta Elena Castillo and her partner Arsenio Alexander Cutín Robich, to teach her the Cuban dances. She also hired four bongo-playing bachelors to keep the beat.[4]

Marta Castillo was a 21-year-old self-taught dancer when Sonja Henie saw her perform for the first time. She had been associated with the Tropicana

[1] Unknown, «Sonja Henie vil lage tredimensjonal skøytefilm.»
[2] Andersen, *Som i en drøm – Sonja Henies liv*, 105.
[3] Strait, *Queen of Ice, Queen of Shadows. The unsuspected life of Sonja Henie*, 237.
[4] Ibid., 239.

and Sans Soucí clubs since her late teens. Coincidence led to her becoming a dancer. As a young singer, she met the Cuban musician Facundo Rivero.

"He asked if I would like to become a dancer and I said yes," laughs Marta, now 89. "Sonja came to Havana in 1952 and saw our show at the Sans Soucí. Afterwards, she met Alexander and me and promised to take us on the tour with her."

The dance became part of Henie's show and the two Cuban dancers were invited onto the tour. In her autobiography, *My Life's Adventures*, Henie wrote:

> They formed a clear focal point and I was fascinated by their lively movements, their characterful faces and assured musical sense. I hired them on the spot and was fortunate because they were just coming to the end of a contract. But by hiring them I also placed a burden on my own shoulders, no matter how pleasant and interesting it might have been. I took the opportunity to learn the special dances and many others. It would be of little use if I, who was to set up the entire revue, didn't know each number from top to toe. With that, Marta and Alexander's dance on the floor became the introduction to the dance on the ice, which took a long time to learn. Now I'm happy I took the couple with me. For me, it was one of the greatest successes I've ever had. Every dancer in the ballet goes through a long period of study. We can't settle for anything but the very best.[5]

Canada bites

Although Cuba was a success for Sonja Henie, it did not provide her with the financial upswing she had hoped for. Once back in the United States and faced with paying the salaries of the 150 staff who kept the wheels turning, she had the choice either to sell her jewellery or take out a loan against her life insurance policy. For Henie, her jewellery was as dear to her as her own family. Her secretary Dorothy Stevens persuaded her to go for option number two.[6] When the opportunity for a new tour in Canada opened up, she said yes. She was unaware that the first stop, St Andrews by-the-Sea, was a small fishing town and that the ice rink had just 600 seats. Sonja gave them the show of their lives – no one could say she was anything but professional.

The tour went from small town to small town and Sonja Henie gave it her all. It would all turn out to be worth it. In New York, the international impresario Morris Chalfen was keeping an eye on Henie and her tour. He was the founder of the concept *Holiday on Ice* and offered her a place on the European tour. At that time, no one else was doing ice shows on the other side of the Atlantic and he had huge success and access to the largest arenas.

Chalfen was planning a longer tour with stops in Paris, London and Berlin, among other places, but when he mentioned Oslo, Henie balked – she couldn't go there. She feared the Norwegian public would boo her and that she would never be forgiven for working to support the American troops without also showing similar public support to Norway during the war.[7]

[5] Henie, *Mitt livs eventyr*, 16-17.
[6] Andersen, *Som i en drøm – Sonja Henies liv*, 115.

Cuban dance during the coronation

Chalfen didn't give up. He had a hunch that this could be a great homecoming and a highlight of Henie's career, and suggested that he could go to Oslo in advance to gauge the mood. The tour started at the Palais des Sports in Paris before moving on to London in June for the coronation of Queen Elizabeth II. She also brought her new number to Europe with her: Cuban Voodoo Ritual with Marta Castillo and Alexander Cutín Robich. They danced on a specially built platform on the ice while Sonja Henie skated around them.

On 2 June 1953, Sonja Henie's ice show opened at Empress Hall with the British royal family in attendance for the premiere. In an earlier interview with Rosa Marquetti Torres, Castillo described the experience of dancing for the future queen: "We were very young and although we knew who she was and what it meant to be Queen of England, we didn't give her the importance I would give her today."[8]

After six weeks in London, the show went on to Berlin. According to Castillo, all the travelling, which included an entourage of just under two hundred people and a mountain of luggage, went without a hitch.

"Everyone was so disciplined. It was so impressive to travel around with Sonja Henie's show. It was a wonderful experience that I will never forget. Sonja was an incomparable performer. And as a boss, I found her humble and sociable. Especially with me," she said.

At the same time, Castillo wished to emphasise that it was hard work.

"People probably think we had a lot of fun along the way, but that's not quite true. We had to be very strict and disciplined with ourselves, and if we had free time we either spent it resting or exploring the city we were in. Most of the time was spent performing and then we had to travel on to a new place."

Centre of attention in Oslo

When Sonja Henie's ensemble arrived in Oslo with the "Sonja Henie train" from Berlin via the Soviet-controlled zone on 18 August 1953, they were met by a large press corps. Eight whole carriages were needed to transport the ensemble's luggage. *Aftenposten* interviewed Marta Castillo on the platform about how the previous shows in Berlin had been received:

> "We were standing on the ice for almost half an hour after the final performance," says the fresh-looking Cuban Marta, who, together with her Alexander, dances a voodoo dance in a big Cuban number. "We have certainly never experienced anything like it. Or perhaps Oslo will beat the record," she says with a brilliant smile revealing a perfect row of pearly whites.[9]

Dagbladet reported that "what attracted most attention on the platform was the fantastic dance couple Marta and Alexander, coloured and beautiful, like ebony."[10]

[7] Ibid., 127.

[8] Torres, «Marta Castillo: the girl in the picture.» 03.03.201 http://www.desmemoriados.com/martha-castillo-la-muchacha-de-la-foto/.

[9] Unknown author, «'Sonja Henie-toget' til Oslo idag. Ingen vanskeligheter med russerne.»

Meanwhile, VG wondered about their experience on the ice:

> Somewhat beyond one's expectations was the encounter with two black-brown Cubans in the ensemble. These are Marta Costillo and Alexander Cutting [sic]. They do not skate, as we first thought, but rather dance barefoot on the ice. And that alone sounds difficult enough.
> "Do you have ice in Cuba?" one pressman asked.
> "Only in cocktails," laughed Alexander Cutting. "But Sonja managed to make artificial ice on the field when she visited us."
> "How long have you been involved?"
> "A year."[11]

After escaping the press, the Cuban dancers were lodged at Hotel Viking.

Joyful dance

When reading the press reports through 2021's eyes, you might say that Sonja Henie struck gold when it came to bringing something "exotic" to Oslo, but from today's perspective, this is open to criticism. Likewise, one may ask whether this was Henie's ulterior motive or whether it was simply the dancer within Sonja Henie who fell head over heels for a new type of dance that inspired and challenged her to push herself forward as a performer. During the rehearsal at Jordal Arena, VG appeared again to strike up a conversation with Castillo and Cutín Robich. "Ice doesn't scare them" boomed the headline:

> Alexander and Marta are one of the sharpest numbers in Sonja Henie's Show. They are two Cubans who want to show us the Voo-Doo Dance and who can stand the ice and cold barefoot. This morning, VG took them to an early training session at Jordal, but there was little enthusiasm between them.
> "Are you crazy?" said Alexander. "We don't walk out onto the ice."
> "But what are you dancing on then?"
> "We have a platform..."
> "And it's not cold...?"
> "It's cold as ice, but we manage it all the same."
> "But what exactly is the Voo-Doo that you dance?"
> "It's a ritual dance with religious meaning. We try to express our joy in simple, expressive movements – and hope people around the world will understand us."[12]

After three days of strained nerves about the weather forecast and the reception in Sonja's hometown, it was time for the premiere.

[10] Unknown author, «Sonjas spesialtog kom i formiddag.»
[11] Unknown author, «Sonja-truppen i Oslo.»
[12] Unknown author, «Is skremmer dem ikke.»

The homecoming

21 August 1953: A small figure tiptoes behind the stage curtain. Eleven thousand people are ready in the outdoor venue at Jordal Arena. It has been raining all day, but the skies are now beginning to clear. Sonja Henie, the woman who has conquered everything – the world championships, the Olympics, Hollywood – is nervous. She is about to try to reconquer her hometown. This iron-willed woman now feels more like Bambi on the icy surface. On her shoulders, her ermine cape hangs heavy. She can hear the audience's response to the skaters in the number before hers. And then it falls quiet. The announcer can be heard over the PA system: "And now, Sonja!" She takes a deep breath and glides out onto the ice.

At Jordal Arena, Sonja Henie was greeted by cheers. The audience was elated that she had finally journeyed home to Norway with her ice revue to serve up some glamour and perform a show without equal in their somewhat dismal, post-war lives. The family of the Crown Prince were sitting in the stands with woollen blankets over their laps. "I actually never suffer from nerves, but there was so much rushing and fussing going on inside me,"[13] she writes in her autobiography. For Henie, Norwegians were astute judges of figure skating and she was unsure whether her show version would be to their taste. Her absence during the Second World War was another worry.

> Today I have no idea what was going through my mind in the last half hour before I stuck my head out between the curtains; I do know that the voice in the loudspeakers said my name in excited anticipation and all of a sudden there I was, out on the ice... All I know is that I quickly felt that I really was home again with my own people, no matter how long I've been a citizen of another country.[14]

The Cuban dancers took to the stage as the final number in the first act. They wore African-inspired animal-skin costumes and had animal teeth hanging from a chain around their necks. The ice made the platform freezing cold beneath their feet, but the rhythms kept them warm. Marta Castillo was the dancer, and Alexander Cutín Robich the sorcerer. Cuban Voodoo Ritual was a number based on the choreography Sonja Henie had first seen in Havana, "an intense union between the cool north and the warm-blooded south".[15] On the ice, Henie danced around the couple in glitter and feathers in her role as goddess.

> Reviewers were impressed by the skating queen's new dance skills: With an all-conquering spirit, adept rhythm and genuine familiarity, she and the artist couple Alexander-Martha served up a dance of the highest quality. Yes – it would be most incorrect to say Sonja has not put in as much work into this dance training as her determined efforts for Olympic gold! This is why regular skating has had to step aside in favour of dance. Sonja has experienced the pleasure of being able to expand her figure skating programme, elevating it further towards the pinnacle of the art in a way that no other figure skater has so far managed.

[13] Henie, *Mitt livs eventyr*, 15.
[14] Ibid, 15.
[15] Ibid., 19.

> Few people will have any notion of quite what it takes in terms of training to perform several minutes of dance performance on the picks of her skates without putting a single foot wrong."[16]

However, not everyone was equally thrilled with Sonja Henie's new dance skills. Håkon Stenstadvold was not impressed. Under the headline "New Baroque age or elephantiasis in the pleasure organs?" he wrote in *Aftenposten*:

> But it is only with the Cuban fire dance that the ice show runs into its first hopeless conflict. The fire dance is a mixture of religion and erotic ecstasy. We are first given a performance by a Cuban dance pair, who of course dare not show anything to do with eroticism or religion. But imagine this sun-drenched, serpentine eroticism taking place on ice with sharpened steel skates! It is a sorry sight in my eyes. All the heat and danger is gone, and we simply sit there, mouths agape: this is truly awkward![17]

Sonja weather

Before they arrived in Oslo, Sonja Henie was unsure how they would be received by the weather gods, since Jordal Arena had no roof. As she wrote in her book, the show made use of expensive costumes that would not withstand the rain; in any case, rain would be a depressing backdrop to what was supposed to be a colourful, joyous show. Against all odds, the weather stayed in their favour every single day.[18] They were forced to cancel on only one occasion. This was given the name "Sonja weather". It was the first time Sonja Henie had danced outdoors since 1936.[19]

"It was absolutely wonderful," says Marta Castillo. "I cannot compare it to any of the other cities on the tour. Sonja's hometown brought out the best in her. I didn't have much free time to see the city, but it was Sonja's home country and people were very kind to us. Alexander and I appreciated the hospitality. But it was freezing cold!"

During the five weeks they were in Oslo, over 350,000 Norwegians came to see Sonja Henie's ice revue over the course of 33 shows. They came from all over the country, with special buses laid on for the trip. Even King Haakon made an appearance and handed Sonja red roses after her performance.

It came to an end on 20 September. The newspapers wrote nothing about the disappointing war years, when Oslo's heroine was conspicuous by her absence. During those weeks, she was embraced as the show woman she was, who had brought a very special performance home to Oslo. In the London show programme one could read about the effort Sonja Henie had made for Norway during the war. When *Aftenposten* visited the show in May 1953, they wrote the following: "By the way, one of the pages was devoted to lauding Sonja's great efforts for the Norwegian underground movement during the war, so be aware of that."[20] And when Kåre Pettersen in *Østlands-Posten* saw the London show, he saw fit to write about precisely this aspect of the programme: "Many will be displeased to read that 'during the last war she contributed generously to the

[16] *Morgenposten*, – som danserinne, 22 August 1953.
[17] Stenstadvold, «Ny barokk-tid eller elefantsyke i fornøyelsesorganene?»
[18] Hoel, Sonja Henie, 59.
[19] Ibid., 57.

Norwegian underground, which fought the Germans. She also gave funds to Norwegian sailors in New York who were stranded there when Germany occupied Norway.' But that kind of thing looks good in a programme, especially in England."[21] When the programmes became available for the Oslo performances, the offending text had been removed and replaced with information about her sport and film achievements.

Danced around the world

After the European tour, Marta Castillo and her dance partner Alexander Cutín Robich returned to Cuba before being invited on a new European tour with the American singer and dancer Josephine Baker. From then on it never stopped, and Marta Castillo ended up travelling around the world as a dancer. Today, Castillo lives in Madrid, but still remembers the tour with Sonja Henie. And after a long life in show business, her day only begins in the evening and the late hours of the night. During the day, she sleeps.

Sources

Andersen, Alf C.. *Som i en drøm – Sonja Henies liv*. Oslo: Chr. Schibsted Forlag, 1985.

Frøisland, Anne Marie. «Sonja-premiére i London – Show for alle pengene.» *Aftenposten*. 26.05.1953.

Henie, Sonja. *Mitt livs eventyr*. Oslo: Gyldendal Norsk Forlag, 1953.

Hoel, Merete Lie. *Sonja Henie*. Oslo: Grøndahl og Dreyers Forlag A/S, 1992.

Pettersen, Kåre. «Sonja Henie og hennes fantastiske kjempeshow.» *Østlands-Posten*. 13.08.1953.

Stenstadvold, Håkon. «Ny barokk-tid eller elefantsyke i fornøyelsesorganene?». *Aftenposten*. 19.09.1953.

Strait, Raymond & Leif Henie. *Queen of Ice, Queen of Shadow. The Unsuspected Life of Sonja Henie*. Chelsea: Scarborough House / Publishers, 1990.

Torres, Rosa Marquetti. «Marta Castillo: La muchacha de la foto.» 03.03.2021. http://www.desmemoriados.com/martha-castillo-la-muchacha-de-la-foto/

Unknown author. «Is skremmer dem ikke.» VG. 19.08.1953.

Unknown author, «'Sonja Henie-toget' til Oslo idag. Ingen vanskeligheter med russerne.» *Aftenposten*. 18.08.1953.

Unknown author. «Sonja Henie vil lage tredimensjonal skøytefilm.» *Dagbladet*. 21.05.1953.

Unknown author. «Sonjas spesialtog kom i formiddag.» *Dagbladet*. 18.08.1953.

Unknown author. «Sonja-truppen i Oslo.» VG. 18.08.1953.

Øy. Vik., «Sonja erobret Oslo på ny - som danserinne.» *Morgenposten*. 22.08.1953.

Muntlig kilde:

Marta Elena Castillo

[20] Frøisland, «Sonja-premiére i London – Show for alle pengene.»
[21] Pettersen, «Sonja Henie og hennes fantastiske kjempeshow.»

Sonja Henie
1953
ICE REVUE
SOUVENIR PROGRAMME

↑

In the box

After seeing Marta Castillo and Alexander Cutín Robich dance at the Sans Soucí nightclub in Cuba, Sonja Henie decided to invite them on the tour with her ice show *Sonja Henie's Dance Revue* in 1952. Here the contract is being signed. Photo: Monagas © 2021 Colección Gladys Palmera.

siste nytt

IS SKREMMER DEM IKKE

←

Dance on ice

When Sonja Henie brought two Cuban dancers home to Oslo with her in 1953, it caused a big stir and they were pursued by an eager press corps. VG joined Marta and Alexander for rehearsals at Jordal Arena ahead of the opening performance. Facsimile: VG/Henie Onstad archive.

→

Trio

Marta Castillo, Sonja Henie and Alexander Cutín Robich pose for the photographer in Cuba, 1952. Note that Marta and Alexander danced without skates. Photo: Unknown © 2021 Colección Gladys Palmera.

→

Tenacious perfectionist

Sonja Henie fell in love with Caribbean rhythms during her stay in Cuba, and she decided to learn to skate the dances on the spot. As she herself said, "Marta and Alexander's dance on the floor became the introduction to the dance on the ice, which took a long time to learn. Now I'm happy I took the couple with me. For me, it was one of the greatest successes I've ever had". Photo: Henie Onstad archive.

←

Ice dance in the theatre

In Havana, Sonja Henie's ice revue was adapted for the stage at Teatro Blanquita. Usually the shows were adapted to arenas with audiences on all four sides, but now it would be taking place on a stage in front of a consolidated audience. The poster announces the final week of the show's run. Facsimile: Henie Onstad archive.

During the last war Miss Henie contributed generously to the Norwegian underground, which fought the Germans. She also gave funds to Norwegian sailors in New York who were stranded there when Germany occupied Norway.

In private life Sonja Henie is the wife of Mr. Winthrop Gardiner, Jr., prominent aviator and noted business executive.

Visiting service hospitals in the U.S.A., and a trip behind the front lines visiting advance hospitals found Miss Henie busy in war work. The entire proceeds of the opening of her 1952 Ice Revue went to the Damon Runyon Cancer Fund and the Womans Auxiliary of the Youth Guidance Center of San Francisco.

←

The English programme

When the *Ice Revue* visited London in 1953, it was possible to read all about Sonja Henie's efforts for Norway during the war. Kåre Pettersen *Østlands-Posten* thought it best to rewrite precisely this page when the show arrived in Oslo later that year: "Many will be displeased to read that 'during the war she contributed generous support to the Norwegian underground movement in their fight against the Germans.'" Facsimile: Henie Onstad archive.

→

Altered text

When the Norwegian programme went on sale during the performances in Oslo, the text had been removed and replaced with information about Sonja Henie's sports and film achievements and the story of how she landed her lucrative film deal in the United States. Facsimile: Henie Onstad archive.

I begynnelsen av 30 årene var det flere filmselskaper som var ute etter Sonja, men den unge dame fant ikke selv tiden moden ennu. Hun hadde satt seg sine mål. Men etter det tredje olympiske mesterskap og det tiende verdensmesterskap i 1936 fant hun tiden inne og dermed sværmet også filmagentene omkring henne. Hun dro til Amerika etter sine triumfer, ga oppvisninger i veldedig øyemed, fikk en enorm presse og gjennom aviskongen Heart ble hun så engagert til to oppvisninger i Los Angeles, så sent som 7. og 9. mai 1936. Dit kom en rekke av filmens berømtheter og også noen direktører. En av dem, direktør for Fox-selskapet, viste sin interesse og kom med et tilbud, som Sonja straks avslo. Hva kan jeg tilby, spurte direktøren. — Hovedrollen, svarte Sonja.

Noen dager etter kom Fox-direktøren tilbake med en fin fem års kontrakt, men Sonja fikk samtidig puttet inn at hun hadde rett til å gi egne forestillinger, når tiden tillot det. Vi fikk filmer, bl. a. «One in a Million», «Thin Ice» og «Happy Landing». Etter de fem årene startet hun sitt eget selskap med verdens største ice-show. — Hun har alltid visst hva hun har villet, Sonja.

↑

Royal visit to the green room

Sonja Henie's Ice Revue was shown for five weeks and 33 performances at Jordal Arena in Oslo. Over 350,000 Norwegians came to experience the icon in the flesh. They came from all over the country and even had special buses laid on. Even King Haakon showed up to hand Sonja Henie red roses after the performance. She described it as afterwards as "a wonderful memory of a truly royal evening". Photo: Henie Onstad archive.

←

Sonja Henie Ice Revue

No feathers or any other decorations were spared when Sonja Henie's costumes were being designed. Photo: Henie Onstad archive.

→

Show frontstage and back...

...was one of the headlines in *Morgenbladet*. A number of prominent guests visited the green room to congratulate Sonja. Here, Crown Princess Martha and Crown Prince Olav greet Sonja Henie after the premiere. Photo: Henie Onstad archive.

→

Interest in art

"The different restructuring processes, from figure skating to film, ice shows and my private life, have often been very difficult. All of these developments require wholehearted effort: work – hard work. I like to envision a common thread between the ballet, figure skating and film work. Perhaps one can trace that interest further into the visual arts, where colour, movement and construction merge." Sonja Henie in *Budstikka*, 23 June 1967. Photo: Henie Onstad archive.

↑

People you believe in

"Art dealers are often bigger than the artists. It is almost an honour to be able to buy pictures from certain art dealers. Often it's quite ridiculous, you ask after a picture, they look you up and down and reply: 150,000 dollars! It's like they're looking at a bag of candy. But the artists are pleasant and we have many good friends among them, Soulages, Hartung, Bazaine, Max Ernst and many young people who very few are aware of yet, but whom we follow and believe in. That's what's the most fun of all, to pursue it, to pursue people you believe in." Sonja Henie in *Aftenposten*, 3 November 1960. Photo: Henie Onstad archive.

→

Jean Bazaine

Dans l'arbre ténébreux, 1957. 162 x 114 cm. Purchased in connection with the exhibition at Kunstnernes Hus in Oslo, 1963. The Henie Onstad collection. © Jean Bazaine/ BONO 2021. Photo: Øystein Thorvaldsen.

ART

She never sat on the fence. As an art collector,
Sonja Henie got straight to the point.

Text: Caroline Ugelstad

In 1958, Sonja Henie visited the Hahn Gallery on Madison Avenue in New York. Stephen Hahn was an American art dealer and collector and an expert on Pablo Picasso and Edgar Degas. We can imagine Henie the style icon entering the gallery, where she quickly bought Picasso's *Femme assise dans un fauteuil* (Woman in an Armchair), painted in 1941.[1] At this point, Sonja Henie's career as a skating star had come to an end, but she was just setting out as an art collector. The purchase at Hahn Gallery tells us something about how quickly and calculatedly she approached her new vocation. Picasso's painting was an innovative painting for its time and it must have been expensive. Is it a portrait of the artist Dora Maar, who was Picasso's muse and mistress during this period? Or is it a reaction to the Spanish Civil War as Picasso had depicted it four years earlier in his renowned work *Guernica* (1937)?

When Henie Onstad Kunstsenter opened its doors in 1968, the picture caused sensation and resentment. However, there is little doubt that the acquisition gave the Henie Onstad collection a great boost. Today, the painting is a cornerstone of the collection, loaned out and reviewed numerous times.

Fifty years of French art

When their foundation was established in 1961, Sonja Henie and Niels Onstad incorporated a hundred paintings from their own collections. When Henie Onstad Kunstsenter opened its doors in 1968, the collection had grown further. Over the centre's lifetime the collection has continued to grow and branch out in different directions. Today, five broadly defined groupings highlight some of the main trends in the collection: the dialogue with Surrealism, CoBrA art, geometric abstraction with directions such as concrete art and op-art, lyrical abstraction in painting and the international network Fluxus. But the heart of the collection was defined by Sonja Henie and Niels Onstad.

Henie's interest in art and collecting gained momentum after she met Niels Onstad (1909-1978) in 1955. Onstad had long been interested in visual art. His mother was a painter and his older brother, Haakon Onstad, collected art. The two brothers also discussed and bought art together. In his private apartment in Manhattan in New York, Onstad had pictures by Edvard Munch and a number of French artists such as Pierre Bonnard, Juan Gris and Fernand Lèger. It was through her relationship with Onstad that Henie's interest in art was also shaped. She had several older, figurative landscape paintings on the walls of her house on Delfern Drive in Beverly Hills, but sold these paintings quickly, before she and Onstad fully embraced contemporary art. "I owned pictures by Rubens, Gainsborough and Renoir, but have now replaced them with the painters of our own time. I feel familiar with them - not in all their forms, but especially the French school", as Henie put it in her own words.[2] After her many achievements in the arena of sport, she took on a new world where artists, gallery owners, curators and museum directors would become her new social circle.

According to Henie Onstad's first director, Ole Henrik Moe (1920–2013), it was natural that it was French art and especially the Paris School that became important to Sonja Henie and Niels Onstad.[3]

[1] The second Picasso painting in the collection, *Femme assise dans un fauteuil* (Woman in an armchair), also from 1941 and with a similar motif, was bought by Niels Onstad at Galerie Bénézit in Paris.
[2] Asker & Bærums Budstikke 23. juni 1967.
[3] Moe, O.H.:1968-1988, s.39.

The Paris School was a loose grouping of young artists who lived, worked and exhibited in Paris in the decades between 1900 and 1970 and who sought new pictorial forms of expression. In retrospect, it is surprising that after thirty years in the United States, Henie did not also turn towards American art. These were the years when, after Paris, New York was becoming the art centre of the world. Neither Henie nor Onstad was enthusiastic about American pop art or the abstract expressionism that dominated American art in the decades after the Second World War. We can assume that after many years in the United States, Henie now wished to promote her European roots and her Norwegianness again. However, the main reason was probably artistic preferences and the collectors' orientation towards the classical and aesthetic. They were looking for "[that] which can delight the eye and provide peace of mind, and at the same time lift one beyond time and place", wrote director Ole Henrik Moe in connection with the opening of the art centre in 1968.[4] They found this in the Paris School artists, who all worked with a decorative and lyrical abstraction of nature. The *Guardian* aptly described the Henie Onstad collection as it was shown at the Tate Gallery in London in 1962:

> There is no desperation, fear or brutality here, there is an exclusively controlled joy in painting, and personal dissonances are excluded. This is somewhat unexpected for those of us who relate the Nordic countries with Gothic barbarism.[5]

As a whole, Henie and Onstad's collection puts fifty years of French art on display. The oldest artists in the collection, such as Jacques Villon, Juan Gris, Pierre Bonnard and Henri Matisse, laid the foundation for the younger artists they collected. From the Paris School they acquired pieces by artists such as Jean Bazaine, with whom Onstad and Henie eventually became close friends, Maurice Estève, Roger Bissière, Alfred Manessier and Gustave Singier.
In addition, they concentrated on the Nordic expressionism that we find in the influential European artist collective CoBrA (1949–1952) with artists such as Karel Appel, Christian Dotremont and Asger Jorn. Sonja Henie, for example, bought seven pictures by Jorn. She also acquired Norwegian artists such as Jakob Weidemann, Anna-Eva Bergman, Jens Johannessen and Gunnar S. Gundersen. Henie and Onstad were the first private collectors in the country to invest heavily in recent works by these four artists. Henie bought as many as eighteen works by Weidemann, several of them masterpieces, such as *Storfuglen letter* (1959) and *Veien til Jerusalem* (1965).

Among advisors

Characteristic of Sonja Henie and Niels Onstad's collection work is the close contact they had with the artists themselves. They were inquisitive collectors who visited artists' studios and enjoyed dealing directly with the artists with whom they established close friendships. However, the Henie Onstad collection was also built up as a result of close dialogue with advisors. Henie and Onstad had four

[4] Moe, O.H.:1968.
[5] Dagbladet, 2. mars 1962.

advisors in particular who were important to them. In the post-war period, the art historian Henning Gran (1906–1978) was the most important advocate of French art in Norway. In the late 1940s and into the 1950s, Gran often travelled to Paris and established contacts with artists and gallery owners. He aided several Norwegian collectors such as Ragnar Moltzau and Rolf Stenersen and contributed to both Jean Bazaine and Alfred Manessier being purchased by the National Gallery in 1950 and 1951, respectively, but he was particularly important to Henie and Onstad. Gran and eventually Ole Henrik Moe, who spoke fluent French, both worked tirelessly for cultural exchange between France and Norway. Among other things, they arranged exhibitions that became important contributions to improving bilateral knowledge and cooperation, such as the exhibition 'French paintings in Norwegian ownership' at Oslo Kunstforening in 1953.

As intendant at Kunstnernes Hus from 1958 to 1962, the painter and professor Alf-Jørgen Aas (1915–1981) also helped to make French art better known in Norway. Aas arranged three large solo exhibitions by French artists at Kunstnernes Hus: Jacques Villon in 1959, Maurice Estève in 1961 and Jean Bazaine in 1963. Onstad and Henie bought several pictures by these artists. Alongside Gran, Moe and Aas, Jakob Weidemann (1923–2001) became an important advisor to Sonja Henie. Weidemann lived in Sweden during the Second World War. He knew European contemporary art well and drew Henie's attention to artists such as Hans Hartung and Pierre Soulages. Henie owned seven paintings by each of these artists, with the great works by Soulages being especially bold purchases.

Self-made

There were a few other female art collectors in Sonja Henie's time, such as the American author Gertrude Stein (1874–1946), Gertrude Vanderbilt Whitney (1875–1942) and Peggy Guggenheim (1898–1979), but the majority were and still are men. Gertrude Stein, who became a close friend of Picasso, created a significant collection of French art together with two of her brothers, Leo and Michael Stein. The collection was sold before and during the Second World War so that it was later scattered between many hands. Gertrude Vanderbilt Whitney, who was a sculptor, collected American art. In 1929 she offered a donation of five hundred more paintings to the Metropolitan Museum of Art. The gift was rejected and she subsequently established her own Whitney Museum in Greenwich Village in 1931. The museum has moved several times, but Whitney's large collection of American art has always been the starting point for the museum's work, not least the Whitney Biennale. Peggy Guggenheim collected American and European art. When she showed her collection at the Venice Biennale in 1948, it was the first time Jackson Pollock and Mark Rothko were presented to a European audience.

The year after Henie Onstad opened its doors at Høvikodden, in 1969, Guggenheim put her own collection on display at the Guggenheim Museum in New York. It is not known if she ever met Sonja Henie, but the two female collectors must have known about each other. Unlike Henie, who became an art collector after a career as a figure skater and businesswoman, art was a way of life for Peggy Guggenheim. She lived and worked in the art scene and was behind several galleries such as Galerie Jeune in London and Art of this Century in New York. Shortly before she died, Guggenheim's home in Venice was made into the Peggy Guggenheim Collection, a museum where her entire collection can now be found on display.[6]

Common to the three women – Stein, Whitney and Guggenheim – is that they acquired art with inherited funds and that they were intimate with art either by being artists themselves or by living in close quarters to artists. Sonja Henie's work as an art collector was different. She was "self-made" and had built her own fortune. She made decisions quickly, never wavered, and built her collection in a short time. Her competitive and business instincts led the way.

Decisions about how and where the collection was to be displayed and managed were made just as quickly. The fact that Henie and Onstad were able to make such quick decisions was, in retrospect, a big plus. Sonja Henie died at a young age, only a year after Henie Onstad Kunstsenter opened, but was able to experience what she had created alongside Onstad during an intense career as an art collector and patron of the arts: one of the largest private donations ever given to the country.

The gift

In 1959, following a request from Kunstnernes Hus in Oslo, Henie and Onstad decided to make the collection accessible to the public. The following year, an extensive touring exhibition began which, over the course of two years, put the collection on display at seventeen key institutions in Norway, Sweden, Denmark, Germany, England, France, Austria and Switzerland. The tour gave Henie and Onstad first-hand knowledge of modern art institutions around the world, and it garnered public attention for the collection. Here at home, making the collection available meant that the public were given the opportunity to encounter art rarely promoted by the National Gallery in Norway. Internationally, the collection attracted a great deal of attention. When the tour arrived at the Tate Gallery in London, Princess Margaret, Queen Elizabeth II's sister, went to visit.
The princess was thrilled with a picture by the artist Jean de Moal, whereupon Sonja spontaneously exclaimed "If you like it, you must take it with you".[7]

It was in the late 1950s that Henie and Onstad decided to set up two foundations that could take care of their collections. In 1961, the documents were formally signed, with the first donation of works being made in 1963. Further works were transferred later on, even after Sonja's death in 1969. Henie and Onstad's exceptional donation was celebrated, but they also encountered pointed criticism and opposition. It was 1968, the year of uprisings. The summer before a fantastic firework display lit up the brand new art centre at Høvikodden, the world was dominated by student revolt. Politically engaged students in major cities, such as New York and Buenos Aires, rebelled against contemporary society, against the US war in Vietnam, and against the French education and examination system. Shortly before, the world had been shaken by the assassination of Martin

[6] Guggenheim museet er en del av The Solomon R. Guggenheim Foundation.
[7] «Sonja gir maleri til prinsesse Margaret», i Dagbladet, 2. mars 1962.

Luther King. Shortly thereafter, student leader Rudi Dutschke was shot in the head during a demonstration in West Berlin. Here at home, the Henie Onstad Kunstsenter, with its Paris School and its French painters, seemed to some Norwegian artists as the pinnacle of a bourgeois, high-brow culture while culturally conservative forces in turn described the centre as "a madhouse with no criteria for quality".[8]

In October 1969, one year after the art centre had opened, Sonja Henie and Niels Onstad travelled to Paris to consider further purchases for the collection. On the way home, Henie died. Shortly afterwards, in November 1969, the centre opened an exhibition in her memory, presenting the approximately 90 paintings she bought and gave to the museum. Art critic and painter Einar Granum wrote in Asker and Bærums Budstikke:

> Along the walls, inside the glass doors, we encounter the entire twentieth century through a contemporary art more colourful, more exacting and more complete than almost any other collection at our latitude. It is not just the artists who are reflected in these works, but also the collector. Sonja Henie did not choose the half-heartedness of compromise. It was either one or the other, she never sat on the fence.[9]

Sonja Henie and Niels Onstad operated in their own age and were part of their own culture. In our time, it is natural to look at what they did not collect. It is striking that Sonja Henie collected so few women, that Henie and Onstad mainly concentrated on European painting and opted out of art with a political bent. These were collectors who were aesthetically oriented and who made controlled choices. Today, Henie Onstad Kunstsenter thinks differently about the way the collection is developed. One of the centre's strategies is to collect more female artists as well as artists from a broad geographical area. But whether we are looking at what the collection does not contain, dealing with what it does, or working on developing new areas, we always work from a nucleus. As one of very few female collectors in her time, and in step with her husband, Sonja Henie was able to shape an art collection, build a home for it, and ensure that it would be looked after for posterity. It was no minor gift.

Sources:

Andersen, Alf G, *Som i en drøm*, Østerås: Chr. Schibsteds Forlag, 1985

Asker & Bærums Budstikke 23. juni 1967

Asker og Bærums Budstikke, 21. november 1969

Dagbladet, 2. mars 1962

Dearbron, Mary: *Peggy Guggenheim. Mistress of Modernism*, London: Virago Press, 2005

Finborud, Lars Mørch, Mot det totale museum. Henie Onstad Kunstsenter og tidsbasert kunst 1961-2011, Oslo: Press Forlag, 2012

[8] Finborud, L. M.: 2012, s 101.

[9] Asker og Bærums Budstikke, 21. november 1969.

Sonja Henie's art collection

Based on catalogues, letters, lists and records from the time the art centre was created, this list presents an overview of Sonja Henie's art collection. The list is probably incomplete, which can be explained by private nature of the collection. Not all works are or have been part of the Henie Onstad collection.

Pierre Alechinsky, *L'envol*, 1961, 130x208

Pierre Alechinsky, *Agitation Proportionée gelse*, 1961, 110x108

Karel Appel, *Fleurs et animaux*, 1951, 105 x 131,5

Karel Appel, *Le nu bleu*, 1960, 195x130

Martin Barré, *57-100-B*, 1957, 162x130

Willi Baumeister,, 1955, 130x100

Jean Bazaine, *Matin à Belle Ile*, 1963, 24x33

Jean Bazaine, *Premier Mars*, 1963, 14x24

Jean Bazaine, *Paysage* 1950, 65x50

Jean Bazaine, *La clairière*, 1951, 130 x 97

Jean Bazaine, *Dans l'arbre ténébreux*, 1957, 162x114

Beaudin, *La fleur dans la maison*

Albert Bitran, *Le Déclin de l'été*, 1961, 150 x 136

Guillaume Beverloo Corneille, *Ensemble métarmorphique*, 1960, 100x73

Guillaume Beverloo Corneille, *Memoire d'un champ jaune*, 1963, 100 x 73

Guillaume Beverloo Corneille, *Vue sur la vallée*, 1961, 81 x 54

K. F. Dahmen, *Bewegte Zone*, 1961, 110 x 135

Jean Dubuffet, *Lieux et instants*, 1958, 73x93

Max Ernst, *Etude pour explosion dans une église*, 1960, 65x54

Maurice Estève, *Fleuriel*, 1956, 60x73

Maurice Estève, *Fresselines*, 1960, 46x38

Maurice Estève, *La ferme du Breuil*, 1943, 50x65

Maurice Estève, *Puybourdin*, 1960, 73x92

Maurice Estève, *Faverdines*, 1955, 89x130

Maurice Estève, *Mouxelle*, 1959, 81x65

Maurice Estève, *Gentioux*, 1960, 81x100

Maurice Estève, *Ruah*, 1960

Maurice Estève, *Tibetsi*

Jean Fautrier, *L'ilot mauve*, 1956, 89x130

Jean Fautrier, *Striures*, 1960, 33x55

Luis Feito, *195*, 1960, 100x81

Sam Francis, *Blue I*, 1960, 91x73,5

Sam Francis, *Composition*, 1957, 40x80

Leon Gischia, *Femmes au trapeze*, 116x73

Marcel Gromaire, *La joie au village*, 1957, 81x100

Juan Gris, *Femme avec écharpe*, 1924, 41x29

Juan Gris, *Le Journal*, 1918, 60x73

Juan Gris, *La bouteille de bière*, 1925, 46x55

Gunnar S. Gundersen, *Sfære*

Hans Hartung, *T. 1962-L33*, 1962

Hans Hartung, *T. 1965 - H36*, 1965, 49x72

Hans Hartung, *T. 55-13*, 1955, 48x81

Hans Hartung, *T. 56-25*, 1956, 180x136

Hans Hartung, *T 57-13 E.*, 1957, 45x34,5

Hans Hartung, *T 59-1.*, 1959, 45x34

Hans Hartung, *T. 59-2*, 1959, 92x60

Hundertwasser, *Paysage avec abscès (les sept années prospères de la taupe*, 1958/65, 55x45

Hundertwasser, *Haus im Wind*, 1962

Jens Johannessen, *Komposisjon*

Jens Johannessen, *Blå figur*, 1967, 75x75

Asger Jorn, *Communaute de joie*, 1960, 88x70,5

Asger Jorn, *Composition*, 1955, 120x82

Asger Jorn, *Poetisk gratifikasjon*, 1956, 146x114

Asger Jorn, *Langsam Mühelos*, 1958, 81x100

Asger Jorn, *Ma novelle vague*, 89x116

Asger Jorn, *Attention, danger*, 1957, 100x81

Asger Jorn, *Le rossignol monstre*

Wilfredo Lam, *Before Dawn*, 1959, 148x217

Charles Lapicque, *Deux amis sur la gréve*, 1947, 81x55

Charles Lapicque, *Tombeau de Palladio*, 1954, 89x116

Fernand Léger, *Le deux profils*, 1933, 64x50

Fernand Léger, *Les danseuses aux oiseaux*,

1953/54, 130x89

Fernand Léger, *Un arbre sur un fond rouge*, 1954, 65x54

Fernand Léger, *Nature morte aux trois fruits*, 50x65

Magnelli, *Groupe fermé*, 1950, 100x81

Alfred Manessier, *La nuit a St. Jean de Luz*, 1955, 130x162

Alfred Manessier, *Le bouquet*, 1955, 60x73

Joan Miró, *Personnage orageux*, 1940, 81x100

Joan Miró, *Composition bleue*, 1953, 30,5x79

Edvard Munch, *Dame i kurvstol*, 1924-25, 73x101

Le Moal, *Composition*, 116x81

Wilfrid Moser, *Concierge*, 1962, 98x119

Wilfrid Moser, *Le Mariage de Lieutenant Kijé*, 1960, 113x145

Pablo Picasso, *Femme assise dans un fauteuil* , 1941, 100x81

Pablo Picasso, *Les rougets (Nature morte aux poisons)*, 1953, 81x100

Serge Poliakoff, *Composition*, 73x60

Jean-Paul Riopelle, *Composition*, 1952, 130x250

Jean-Paul Riopelle, *Composition*, 1956, 116x89

Jean-Paul Riopelle, *Horizontal black and white painting*, 1953, 73x92

Gérard Schneider, *Composition 6*, 1958, 80x91,5

Gérard Schneider, *Composition 11*, 1956, 130x162

Gustave Singier, *Intérieur en Provence*, 1957, 195x130

Gustave Singier, *Provence*, 1958, 130x97

K. R. H. Sonderborg, *Iceskating at Rockefeller Center. Febr.7*, 1961, 111x70

Pierre Soulages, *Peinture 20. Décembre*, 1958, 195x130

Pierre Soulages, *Peinture 8. Août*, 1958, 89x130

Pierre Soulages, *Peinture 22. Mars*, 1959, 200x265

Pierre Soulages, *Peinture*, 1959, 130x162

Pierre Soulages, *Peinture*, 1954, 81x60

Pierre Soulages, *Peinture*, 1959, 120x130

Pierre Soulages, *Peinture*, 1962, 265x200

Nicolas de Staël, *Composition*, 1946, 73x53

Nicolas de Staël, *Composition No.1*, 1948, 50x61

Nicolas de Staël, *A Piranèse*, 1948, 100x73

Nicolas de Staël, *Agrigente*, 1953, 54x73

Mantra, *Komposisjon*, 57x76

Tamayo, *Nocturne*, 1959, 130x195

Tamayo, *Femme tropique*, 195x130

Thorstein Thorsteinson, *Hane og høne*

Jaques Villon, *Intérieur*, 1954, 81x65

Jaques Villon, *Le cèdre*, 1948, 65x81

Jaques Villon, *Grande maternité*, 1948, 146x115

Jaques Villon, *Panathénées*, 1955, 54x81

Jaques Villon, *Comme il vous plaira*, 1956, 73x92

Fritz Winter, *Trio*, 1956, 114x147

Fritz Winter, *Komposition Rot Gelb*, 1957, 136x146

Jakob Weidemann, *Blå skygger*, 1964

Jakob Weidemann, *Epleblomst*, 1964

Jakob Weidemann, *Interiør*,

Jakob Weidemann, *Oppstilling*, 1959

Jakob Weidemann, *Storfuglen letter*, 1959, 150x200

Jakob Weidemann, *Svart løv*, 1961

Jakob Weidemann, *Anne Maries have*, 1964, 250x450

Jakob Weidemann, *Gutt og rød ball*, 1962

Jakob Weidemann, *Blå skygger*, 1964, 130x210

Jakob Weidemann, *Blomsterhandleren*, 1964, 150x300

Jakob Weidemann, *Høst*, 1963, 80x99

Jakob Weidemann, *Høstløv*, 90x100

Jakob Weidemann, *Gjøglere*

Jakob Weidemann, *Landskap*, 1965, 65x81

Jakob Weidemann, *To løv*, 1959, 180x259

Jakob Weidemann, *Løv og mose*, 1960

Jakob Weidemann, *Rød gren*, 1963, 49x61

Jakob Weidemann, *Rødt løv*, 1960, 99x79

↑

Karel Appel

Le nu bleu/The blue nude, 1960, 195x130 cm. Purchased at Gal. Rive Droite, Paris, 1960. Henie Onstad collection. © Karel Appel/BONO 2021. Photo: Øystein Thorvaldsen.

→

Jean Bazaine

Paysage/Landscape, 1950. 65x50 cm. Henie Onstad collection. © Jean Bazaine/BONO 2021. Photo: Øystein Thorvaldsen.

↑

Sam Francis

Composition, 1957.
40 x 80 cm. Henie Onstad collection. © 2021 Sam Francis Foundation, California/BONO. Photo: Øystein Thorvaldsen.

→

Personal friends

Sonja Henie developed close friendships with several artists. This picture shows the French artist Jean Bazaine, Sonja Henie and Niels Onstad in Oslo, 1963, with inscription. Personable from one: “To Jean, With Love, Sonja”, and a little more strained from the other: “Warm regards, Niels”. Photo: Henie Onstad archive.

↑

Hans Hartung

T. 55-13, 1955, 48x81 cm. Purchased directly from the artist. Henie Onstad collection. © Hans Hartung/ BONO 2021. Photo: Øystein Thorvaldsen.

←

Pierre Soulages

Peinture, 1962, 265x200 cm. Purchased directly from the artist. Henie Onstad collection. © Pierre Soulages/ BONO 2021. Photo: Øystein Thorvaldsen.

↑

Jakob Weidemann

Storfuglen letter, 1959, 150x200 cm. Purchased directly from the artist. Henie Onstad collection. © Jakob Weidemann/ BONO 2021. Photo: Øystein Thorvaldsen.

→

Jakob Weidemann

To løv, 1959, 180x259 cm. Henie Onstad collection. ©Jakob Weidemann/ BONO 2021. Foto: Øystein Thorvaldsen.

←

Distinctive

Photographed on her bed at home in LA with the pointe technique of a ballet dancer, the posture of an elite athlete, and uniquely attired in a woollen hat, pearls and diamonds. Sonja Henie stood out in most settings. Photo: Henie Onstad archive.

←

Karel Appel

Fleurs et animaux/Flowers and animals, 1951, 105 x 131.5 cm. Purchased directly from the artist. Henie Onstad collection. © Karel Appel/ BONO 2021. Photo: Øystein Thorvaldsen.

↑

Maurice Estève

Gentioux, 1960,
81x100 cm. Purchased at Gal. Villand & Galanis, Paris. Henie Onstad collection. © Maurice Estève/ BONO 2021. Photo: Øystein Thorvaldsen.

→

Maurice Estève

Fresselines, 1960,
46x38 cm. Purchased at Gal. Villand & Galanis, Paris. Henie Onstad collection. ©Maurice Estève/ BONO 2021. Photo: Øystein Thorvaldsen.

↑

Max Ernst

Etude pour explosion dans une église / Study for explosion in a church, 1960, 65x54 cm. Purchased at Gal. Arnaud, Paris. Henie Onstad collection. © Max Ernst/BONO 2021. Photo: Øystein Thorvaldsen.

↑

Perfectionist

Sonja Henie built her art collection in record time: "For me it's like this – once I've started I can't stop before I'm satisfied with the result." Sonja Henie in Budstikka, 23 June 1967. Photo: Henie Onstad archive.

→

Asger Jorn

Attention, danger, 1957, 100x81 cm. Purchased at Gal. Benador, Geneve. Henie Onstad collection. © Asger Jorn/BONO 2021. Photo: Øystein Thorvaldsen.

↑

Jens Johannessen

Blå figur, 1967, 75 x 75 cm. Purchased at Galleri Haaken, Oslo, 1967. Henie Onstad collection. © Jens Johannessen/BONO 2021. Photo: Øystein Thorvaldsen.

←

Landøya

Sonja spent every summer, with the exception of wartime, at Landøya in Asker. After she married Niels Onstad, the walls of the house were filled with modern paintings. Photo: Henie Onstad archive.

→

Straight at the camera

Sonja Henie was the most camera-savvy person in the marriage. Photo: Henie Onstad archive.

←

Willi Baumeister

Aru dunkel-Blau, 1955. 131x100 cm. Henie Onstad collection. © Willi Baumeister/BONO 2021. Photo: Øystein Thorvaldsen.

↑

Jean Dubuffet

Lieux et instants / Places and moments, 1958, 73x93 cm. Purchased at Gal. Beyeler, Basel Henie Onstad collection. © Jean Dubuffet/ BONO 2021. Photo: Øystein Thorvaldsen.

→

Hans Hartung

T 1965 - H 36, 1965, 49x72 cm. Signed "To Sonja. Hans 65." Provenance of the artist. Henie Onstad collection. © Hans Hartung/BONO 2021. Photo: Øystein Thorvaldsen.

→

Pablo Picasso

Femme assise dans un fauteuil / Woman in armchair, 1941, 100x81 cm. Purchased at Hahn Gallery, New York. Henie Onstad collection. © Succession Pablo Picasso / BONO 2021 Photo: Øystein Thorvaldsen.

←

Woman in armchair

Sonja Henie liked to compete with her husband, even when it came to buying art. They each bought their own Picasso portrait of Dora Maar. Today her picture is considered a cornerstone of the Henie Onstad collection. Photo: Henie Onstad archive.

→

Hans Hartung

T 59-1., 1959, 45x34 cm. Signed "Pour Sonja Hans Hartung 1959". Provenance of the artist. Henie Onstad collection. © Hans Hartung/ BONO 2021. Photo: Øystein Thorvaldsen.

←

Determined

While Sonja firmly believed that it was Niels who knew the most about art, artists say that she knew what was good – and made quick decisions. According to Jean Bazaine, she would simply say, "I like that" or "I don't like that." Photo: Henie Onstad archive.

↑

Hans Hartung

T. 56-25, 1956, 180x136 cm. Purchased directly from the artist. Henie Onstad collection. © Hans Hartung/ BONO 2021. Photo: Øystein Thorvaldsen.

←

Hans Hartung

T. 59-2, 1959, 92x60 cm. Purchased directly from the artist. Henie Onstad collection. © Hans Hartung/ BONO 2021. Photo: Øystein Thorvaldsen.

↑

Hans Hartung

T 57-13 E., 1957, 45x34.5 cm. Signed "A Sonja Henie très amicalement Hans Hartung". Provenance of the artist. Henie Onstad collection. © Hans Hartung/ BONO 2021. Photo: Øystein Thorvaldsen.

→

Pierre Soulages

Peinture 20. Décembre, 1958, 195x130 cm. Purchased directly from the artist. Henie Onstad collection. © Pierre Soulages/BONO 2021. Photo: Øystein Thorvaldsen.

←

Contemporary

Sonja Henie purchased work from the period in which she lived, and preferably directly from the artists themselves. Still, she had a few historical works in the collection, like this one by Fernand Léger. Photo: Henie Onstad archive.

→

Fernand Léger

Les danseuses aux oiseaux / Dancers with birds, 1953/54, 130x89 cm. Purchased from Saidenberg Gallery, New York. Henie Onstad collection. © Fernand Léger/BONO 2021. Photo: Øystein Thorvaldsen.

F.LEGER-53

↑

Alfred Manessier

Le bouquet / *The bouquet*, 1955, 60x73 cm. Purchased from Coll. Saidenberg, New York. Henie Onstad collection. © Alfred Manessier/BONO 2021. Photo: Øystein Thorvaldsen.

←

Joan Miró

Personnage orageuz / *Stormy person*, 1940, 81x100 cm. Purchased at Hahn Gallery, New York. Henie Onstad collection. ©Succesión Miró / BONO 2021. Photo: Øystein Thorvaldsen.

↑

Joan Miró

Composition bleue / *Blue composition*, 1953, 30.5x79 cm. Purchased at Frank Perls Gallery, New York. Henie Onstad collection. © Succesión Miró / BONO 2021 Photo: Øystein Thorvaldsen.

↑

Where art happens

“The press conference ended with a rehearsal of Arne Nordheim’s ‘Solitaire’, an intense experience about which there were probably divided opinions. But it was an effective demonstration of a museum where art happens.” Sonja Henie in *Dagbladet*, 23 August 1968. Photo: Henie Onstad archive.

→

Nicolas de Staël

Agrigente, 1953, 54x73 cm. Purchased at Gal. Beyeler, Basel. Henie Onstad collection. © Nicolas de Staël/BONO 2021. Photo: Øystein Thorvaldsen.

↖

Juan Gris

Le Journal, 1918, 60x73 cm. Purchased at Pearls Gallery, New York. Henie Onstad collection. © Juan Gris/BONO 2021. Photo: Øystein Thorvaldsen.

↑

Juan Gris,

Femme avec écharpe / Woman with scarf, 1924, 41x29 cm. Purchased at Gal. Benador, Genève. Henie Onstad collection. © Juan Gris/BONO 2021. Photo: Øystein Thorvaldsen.

←

The donors

Sonja Henie and Niels Onstad. Photo: Henie Onstad archive.

→

Jaques Villon

Grande maternité, 1948, 146x115 cm. Purchased at Gal. Louis Carré, Paris. Henie Onstad collection. © Jaques Villon/BONO 2021. Photo: Øystein Thorvaldsen.

JACQUES Villon

↑

Fernand Léger

Le deux profils / The two profiles, 1933, 64x50 cm. Purchased at Frank Perls Gallery, New York. Henie Onstad collection. © Fernand Léger/BONO 2021. Photo: Øystein Thorvaldsen.

↓

The big move

"I owned pictures by Rubens, Gainsborough and Renoir, but have now replaced them with the painters of our own time. I feel familiar with them - not in all their forms, but especially the French school." Sonja Henie in *Budstikka*, 23 June 1967. Photo: Henie Onstad archive.

→

The collecting couple

Sonja and Niels bought pictures together and on their own. Through an organic process, the images were transferred to Sonja Henie and Niels Onstad's foundations in several stages, now constituting the Henie Onstad collection. Photo: Henie Onstad archive.

↑
Jakob Weidemann
Anne-Maries have, 1964. 250 x 450 cm. Henie Onstad collection. © Jakob Weidemann/BONO 2021. Photo: Øystein Thorvaldsen.

↑

The hand of creation

Høvikodden's architecture forms part of the overall legacy Sonja leaves behind. In many ways the building is an extension of the feats she performed on the ice, in business and on film. Two young Norwegian architects, Eikvar and Engebretsen, won the design competition. Facsimile: Byggekunst.

AR CHI TEC TURE

The story of how visionary architectural ideas found their way to Høvikodden

Text: Erik Fenstad Langdalen

In the Norwegian context, the radical project that arose at Høvikodden in 1968, initiated and financed by Sonja Henie and Niels Onstad, was a completely new type of art institution. Moderna Museet, under the innovative directorship of Pontus Hultén, Louisiana Kunstmuseum and its owner-director Knut W. Jensen, and Stedelijk museum under the influential Willem Sandberg were all role models for a new kind of institution that Henie Onstad's director, Ole-Henrik Moe, chose to call the total museum.[1]

The architecture of the art centre, which was conceived by the young architects Jon Eikvar (1933–) and Svein-Erik Engebretsen (1933–), inscribed itself into the artistic project through an open relationship with its surroundings, a flexible spatial organisation, an unconventional form, and innovative material experiments.

A hypermodern facility

When reading Eikvar and Engebretsen's description of their winning project in the journal *Byggekunst* from 1965, one is not struck primarily by its radicalism: "The realisation of the ideas that form the basis of Sonja Henie's and Niels Onstad's Foundations presupposes a building that is suitable for all the many kinds of activities that are unique to modern museums. The building to be erected is intended as the framework for a diverse and highly open museum enterprise, a living and outward-looking institution."[3] Although the text contains an implicit critique of the traditional art museum, which in the Norwegian context at the time was not particularly "modern", "open", "living" or "outward-looking", the description is modest in relation to the publicity the building received when it opened in 1968. "The art centre at Høvikodden: also an experiment in architecture" was *Morgenbladet*'s headline for the newspaper's full coverage of the centre's opening on 23 August 1968.[4] *A-Magasinet*'s Sigurd Hennum described the centre as a "hypermodern facility".[5] *Hardanger Folkeblad* added,

> The idea one is left with when walking around the Henie-Onstad Foundation's magnificent premises at Høvikodden in Bærum is that this building is a work of art in itself. It breaks with all conventional architecture.[6]

When studying the architectural competition's agenda, which was announced on 23 October 1962, there is little evidence of the radicalism to come. Apart from the requirement that the museum should "illuminate trends and ideas in contemporary literature, theatre, film, dance, music, architecture and handicrafts", what is being described is a fairly traditional art museum rather than an art centre.[7] But when studying Eikvar and Engebretsen's competition proposal, submitted by the deadline of 1 April 1963, one glimpses the contours of those qualities that would provide the framework for Ole Henrik Moe's artistic project. The centre's access road, entrance and car park are almost identical to the solution that ended up being built. The fan shape of the floor plan is easily recognisable, but the fan borrows its shape from a bird's wing rather than a chestnut leaf, which was the metaphor employed upon its completion in 1968.[8] The exhibition spaces are not

[1] From a quote by Ole Henrik Moes reproduced in *Arbeiderbladet*, 24 August 1968, in an article penned by the journalist Kjell Johanssen: "De glade givere liker å stå på terskelen til fremtiden".
[2] Finborud, L. 2012.
[3] *Byggekunst* 5 1965: 138-140.
[4] *Morgenbladet*, 23.august 1968.
[5] *A-magasinet*, uketillegg til Aftenposten, 17.august 1968.
[6] *Hardanger Folkeblad* 19.juli 1968.

separated by the high-quality intermediate spaces that characterise today's solution, but are adjacent to one another and bound together by two rows of openings as well as by an outdoor terrace facing the sea. The fan shape is accentuated by large roof beams that lead visitors from the vestibule towards the five exhibition rooms. The text on the floor plan reveals a relatively conventional layout with different rooms for "contemporary art", "the pioneers", "changing exhibitions", "print" and a "children's exhibition". The right-angled administration wing is far larger than it is today, but also contains a library, lecture hall and restaurant. The centre's geometry is continued in the treatment of the terrain in the form of terraces and access paths.

The art centre's distinctive physiognomy

The competition's jury, which included renowned architects such as Trond Eliassen, Herman Krag, Eivind Mostue and Vilhelm Wohlert (the architect behind the Louisiana Kunstmuseum), the artist Alf-Jørgen Aas and the owners themselves, Sonja Henie and Niels Onstad (president of the jury), expressed enthusiasm for Eikvar and Engebretsen's "1212" proposal. Still, they had certain reservations:

> The project is afforded great interest due to its distinctive physiognomy. The exterior perspective and façades are among the most beautiful in the competition and testify to a strong design will and faculty to lend it a personal and persuasive expression. In a fortuitous and distinctive way, the building seems to form part of a whole with the headland's ridge. (...) The plan's principal arrangement is excellent, but it is as if its authors' struggle with the problems of architectural form has left too little energy for a more convincing design of the various spatial groupings. (...) The highly unique design of the exhibition rooms and their connection with the vestibule is the project's essential idea. It is interesting and it may be possible to create an exciting and usable space on this basis, but on this point the burden of proof lies with its proponents. (..) The space for changing exhibitions is weakest, having fallen prey in its entirety to a straitjacketed form.[9]

The jury found none of the 95 submitted drafts worthy of winning, but recommended a second round of competition between the five best proposals from architects Kjell Lund and Niels Slaatto, John Engh, Paal Cappelen and Torbjørn Rodahl, Helge Hjertholm, and Eikvar and Engebretsen.[10]

The jury's general remarks give an insight into the museological discussion that must have taken place during the period of evaluation. They point out the significance of the New York's Museum of Modern Art (MoMA) for the inception of a new museum concept:

> The traditional perception of the museum as an institution for collection and conservation has been shattered. Instead, an outward-looking contact-seeking organism (...) has emerged that considers the

[7] *Norske Arkitektkonkurranser* nr. 99, supplement to *Arkitektnytt* No. 15, 1963.
[8] *Hardanger Folkeblad* 19. juli 1968.
[9] *Norske Arkitektkonkurranser* No. 99.
[10] John Engh collaborated with Kjell Cranner, Hans Chr. Gaaserud, Johan Holter, Bjørn Ljungberg, Carl-Henrik Nøstvik, Jon Seip, Simen Stenseth, Per Sætre and Jon Torleif Voraa.

presentation of art as its essential function, using various means of communication as its natural instruments. (...) [It] would not be unrealistic to imagine that completely new expressions of creative activity will emerge as a result of this meeting between artist and audience.[11]

We also gain an understanding of how the jury imagined these ideas would be incorporated into specific proposals:

In addition to exhibition rooms of varying character, one of which is characterised as a work studio suitable for e.g. theatre and concert use, the museum will be a workplace for students, who on occasion will be able to provide the visiting public with different art research services. This presupposes that different events must be able to take place at the same time and without disturbing each other, e.g. it ought to be possible to show films in the lecture hall, hold a concert in the work studio and exhibit the permanent collection, at the same time as a gala dinner may be held in the restaurant area.[12]

The competition program is radicalised – and the total museum takes shape

During the evaluation period, the conventional competition agenda was elaborated upon and "radicalised", which must have influenced the work of the architects in the competition's second phase.

The five reworked proposals that were submitted by the deadline of 13 December 1963 largely followed the plans made in the first phase, but Eikvar and Engebretsen's winning project had undergone extensive change. In addition to finding space for Sonja Henie's collection of prizes, they had redesigned both the exhibition spaces and the administration wing. A greater proportion of the programme was incorporated into the fan form, and the exhibition spaces were separated from each other. This opened up for a more flexible use, at the same time as it provided a view of the sea from the vestibule. The exhibition spaces acquired their characteristic polygonal shapes and circular skylights (which were later changed to rectangular ones). The ground floor, which in the first phase had been on one level, now stepped up to the west to a section with changing rooms, a bar and grill and events areas. The outdoor facilities were adapted and now included a larger proportion of the site. The jury was enthusiastic and emphasised the proposal's flexibility and scenic qualities: "The central vestibule, where one gets a glimpse of its position in the landscape and an understanding of the division and location of the public area, is a strong move. (...) The main thrust of the project is so good and its artistic spirit so strong that it should be possible to develop it to provide a distinctive, characterful and very well-functioning museum."[13]

As it is presented in *Byggekunst* from 1965, the winning project has been further adapted and, in its floorplan, is almost identical to the project that was completed barely three years later.[14] The vestibule opens towards the

[11] *Norske Arkitektkonkurranser* No. 99.
[12] Ibid.

entrance and the sea to the west to a greater extent than before, the expressive roof beams that remained in the adapted competitive drafts have been removed, and the difference in level in the vestibule follows the building's concentric logic. The spectacular, circular glass elevator and the external amphitheatre are also introduced at this time.

The project would undergo further changes towards its completion in 1968. The experimentation even extended to the construction site, among other things in the form of a 1:1 test room, "electronic data processing" to mark out the buildings on the site, new types of building materials and techniques that reflected both the project's experimental character and the client's generous budget.[15]

Role models

What role models did Eikvar and Engebretsen have for their first competitive proposal, given the relatively conventional competition agenda and in the absence of the radical curatorial ideas that were developed in the competition's wake?

The most obvious reference would be the Louisiana Kunstmuseum in Humlebæk, Denmark, with its rural location and progressive profile, which was inaugurated on 14 August 1958. But whereas Wolhert, its architect, opens the exhibition space to nature, in Norway Eikvar and Engebretsen enclose the art within a controlled environment. The similarity lies in the way they renegotiate the relationship between art and the public by removing the threshold between institution and society, both literally and figuratively. It is not inconceivable that Louisiana played a role in the design of the museum, but as Lars Mørch Finborud has pointed out, "the architects wished by all means to avoid too intimate a relationship with nature":

> When we saw that museum, it struck us that we recalled more about the surroundings than of what we had gone and seen inside the museum itself, it had made a stronger impression on us. And we think it is proper that when a museum is located in such robust nature, as it is here and down at Louisiana, that one is given the opportunity to focus on the pictures and not for them to be diffuse in the impression they leave.[16]

Another natural reference might have been Pontus Hultén's Moderna Museet, which moved into a former military training building on Skeppsholmen on 9 May 1958, but there is little indication that the young Norwegian architects found inspiration there. The close collaboration between Moe and Hultén had a major impact on the conceptualisation and programming of the art centre at Høvikodden, but left few traces in the architects' competitive proposals.

Following the announcement of the winner at Kunstnernes hus on 29 February 1964, the proud winners claimed in an interview for *Aftenposten* that "[they] had not been given direct impulses from any building in particular, but stated that the exhibition of future architecture that they themselves had a part in arranging at the premises of Oslo Architects' Association had been very inspiring."[17]

[13] *Norske Arkitektkonkurranser* No.105, suplement to *Arkitektnytt* No. 12, 1964.
[14] *Byggekunst* 5 1965: 138-140.
[15] Johnsen, E. 2010.
[16] Finborud, L. 2012: 31.

To the question of which international architects they valued most, the answer was "Utzon, the American Kahn, and the old greats". And the article elaborates: "The architects revealed that their chief inspiration was the big three: Frank Lloyd Wright, Le Corbusier and Mies van der Rohe. When asked if they could highlight any Norwegian sources of inspiration, there was a moment of silence before they mentioned Ove Bang's buildings from the 1930s and Norwegian wood architecture."[18]

In terms of the design, it is not easy to find specific role models among the "old greats". The closest are Wright's later projects such as *Dr. and Mrs. Arthur O'Keefe house* (1940s), *Curtis and Lillian Meyer house* (1950–51) and *David and Gladys Wright house* (1950–55).

In the story of the art centre's creation, the architect Alvar Aalto, the fourth of architecture's "old greats", is conspicuous by his absence. If one studies the floor plans of Aalto's Hochhaus in Bremen (1962), early sketches of the library in Rovaniemi (1965) and the cultural centre in Wolfsburg (1959–62), the similarity with Eikvar and Engebretsen's first competition proposal is striking. The art centre is not a copy, but rather a meaningful elaboration of Aalto's architectural ideas.

Another important reference for the art centre's architects may be the world exhibition in Brussels in 1958, which was a formidable showcase for new exhibition architecture.[19] Le Corbusier's organic Phillips Pavilion, Reima Pietelä's stepped wooden pavilion and Sverre Fehn's plastic experiments stand out as possible sources of inspiration. Fehn's Venice Pavilion, which was completed in June 1962, four months before the art centre competition was announced, may also have been important, especially given the key role of Pontus Hultén in its creation.[20] Fehn's description of the Nordic Pavilion in *Byggekunst* in 1962 may give us some hint of the ideas in circulation at the time: "And since the representation of modern art is as complicated and diverse as our surroundings, and art's future path seems to be moving away from architecture, the architect's task becomes for the building's passivity to offer art the greatest freedom possible."[21]

Eikvar and Engebretsen's experiments with concrete are not exceptional for their time; Erling Viksjø's government building (1959) and Lund and Slaatto's Asker town hall (1963) are prominent predecessors. The two architects' role in the design of the Norwegian Telecommunication installation building (1965–66) at Tollbugata in Oslo, as employees of Nils Holter, must have been important. Their interview in *Dagbladet* from 1964 reveals that the architects envisioned an art centre designed in "almost white concrete", but Holter's experiences must have influenced them.[22] The installation building's radical façade leaves its mark on the art centre's bush-hammered and grooved outer wall.

Just as relevant as identifying concrete design forerunners is to establish an understanding of the context in which the architects operated.

Changes in architectural education

Jon Eikvar and Svein-Erik Engebretsen graduated from the State Architecture Programme at the National College of Art and Design (SHKS) in 1959 and were

[17] *Aftenposten* 29 February 1964.
[18] Finborud, L. 2012.
[19] The diploma class on the state architecture programme at SHKS conducted a study trip to the exhibition 4–16 May 1958, when Engebretsen and Eikvar were students there, according to the SHKS annual report 1957–58.
[20] Lending, M. og Langdalen, E 2021.
[21] Fehn, S. 1962.
[22] *Dagbladet*, 29 February 1964. Here they also emphasise the central role that the construction engineer and "concrete expert" Finn Robert Haugli played in the design of the competition proposal. Haugli taught at SHKS.

exposed to ideas circulating among the school's teachers, which in the period 1954–59 included architects such as Knut Knutsen, Arne Vesterlid, Alf Bastiansen and Berent A. Moe as part of the permanent staff, and young architects such as Håkon Mjelva, Christian Norberg-Schulz and Dag Rognlien in "minor positions".[23] Through their training, Eikvar and Engebretsen came into contact with an international architectural discourse. The architectural education at the school was under constant change. A testimony to the reorientation that took place in the mid-1950s is what was known as the AA exhibition, which was held at the school in the autumn of 1956 under the direction of Berent A. Moe and Michael Raymond Lloyd: "a demonstration exhibition with complete teaching materials" from the leading Architectural Association School of Architecture (AA) from which Lloyd had just graduated and where Moe had been working as a teacher for a year.[24] The influential London school hired teachers on short engagements, including people like Maxwell Fry, Le Corbusier, Alvar Aalto, Louis Mumford and Peter Smithson, and was "strongly associated with events in the field." In connection with the exhibition, Lloyd and Moe held a series of lectures and reviews "where they communicated their experiences and opinions in conjunction with SHKS's teaching programme". Immediately after this, department head Knut Knutsen initiated a "new programme layout" for the architectural training at SHKS with AA as a model. Lloyd taught at the Oslo School of Architecture in the period 1962–63 and, as principal at AA in the period 1966–71, had great influence on the international discourse in architecture.[25]

Arne Korsmo, who left his mark on the school as head teacher and head of the wood department in the period 1936–57, had an extensive international network. Collaborating with Jørn Utzon was hugely important in the form of joint projects and involvement in Team 10, the successor to the CIAM association which included architects such as Alison and Peter Smithson, Jaap Bakema, Aldo van Eyck, Georges Candilis, Kenzo Tange, Ralph Erskine, Oscar Hansen, Reima Pietilä, Oswald Mattias Ungers, Giancarlo De Carlo and the Norwegian Geir Grung. The legendary CIAM meeting, which was held at the Kröller-Müller Museum in Ottorlo in September 1959, marked a regime change in architecture and coincided with Eikvar and Engebretsen debuting as architects.

Circulating ideas

To understand the currents that influenced the architectural discourse of the early 1960s, it is tempting to turn to the influential architect, architectural historian and editor Christian Norberg-Schulz, who in his essay "Architecture today" in *Byggekunst* no. 7 1963 attempts to provide an overview of contemporary architecture. In the introduction he quotes from the architectural theorist Sigfried Giedion's Harvard lecture from 1961, which pointed out a prevailing confusion in architecture: "[It] exists in contemporary architecture, as in painting; a kind of pause, even a kind of exhaustion (...) Fatigue is normally accompanied by uncertainty, what to do and where to go." Norberg-Schulz follows up with an assurance that "[today], two years later, we are already beginning to see a way out of the uncertainty Giedion described." In his essay, he points to the shift that

[23] SHKS, annual reports 1954–1955, 1955–1956, 1956–1957, 1957–1958, 1958–1959, 1959–1960.
[24] SHKS, annual report 1956–1957.
[25] ibid.
[26] Norberg-Schulz, C. (1963).

has taken place from the first phase of modernism, with an architecture whose primary aim was to satisfy human physical needs, through what Le Corbusier identified as "the architectural means that could provide us with elemental pleasures: the independent skeleton, the free plan and open façade, and the continuous ground level with differentiated traffic". He further points out that soon after the war a new problem emerged which "expressed itself in the urge for more articulate and varied forms", not least represented by Alvar Aalto's architecture. He quotes the American Paul Rudolph who, in his speech to the alumni students at the School of Architecture at Yale in February 1958, points out the need for a new architecture:

> We need desperately to relearn the art of disposing our buildings to create different kinds of space: the quiet, enclosed, isolated, shaded space; the hustling, bustling space, pungent with vitality; the paved, dignified, vast, sumptuous, even awe-inspiring space; the mysterious space; the transition space which defines, separates, and yet joins juxtaposed spaces of contrasting character. We need sequences of space which arouse one's curiosity, give a sense of anticipation, which beckon and impel us to rush forward to find that releasing space which dominates, which acts as a climax and magnet, and gives direction. Most important of all, we need those outer spaces which encourage social contact.[26]

[27]Rudolph, P. 1958.

Norberg-Schulz draws attention to Le Corbusier's church in Ronchamps and the Finn Reima Pietilä's *Studentkårshus* in Otaniemi. Both architects are able to "translate psychological qualities into three-dimensional form" in "distinctly 'organic' solutions wherein the parts are connected together into great continuous wholes". Other examples of architects he believes work with a system of "collaborative parts" are Walter Förderer, Piet Blom and Louis Kahn. He describes Kahn's *Richards Medical Research Laboratories* at the University of Pennsylvania (1960) as a "group formation" which does not bring together all its functions into one overriding form, but rather links together "a few types of clear volumes that serve quite specific classes of function" and further points out that "the project has had a redemptive effect on many of those who have worked with row, cluster and group formations in order to give the city a new plastic context". He cites Jørn Utzon's project for the world exhibition in Copenhagen in 1959 and Kingohusene in Helsingør (1956) as examples "that adapting to the terrain is not the same as haphazard dissolution of form". Norberg-Schulz regards both Kahn and Utzon's works as "syntheses of Mies van der Rohe's technological architecture and Wright-Aalto's 'organic' intentions." By way of conclusion, Norberg-Schulz tries to translate "recent architecture" into three basic principles. He distinguishes between 1) the potential of mass and space as architectural means of expression, 2) the *open form*, and 3) *theme and variation*, exemplified by Oswald Mattias Unger's *Neue Stadt*, Enrico Castiglioni's railway station project and Sverre Fehn's project for Spiraltoppen, respectively.

Eikvar and Engebretsen's *Aftenposten* tribute to "Utzon, the American Kahn, and the old greats", indicates that they shared the ideas Norberg-Schulz conveys in his essay, which may have left its mark on the open "group formation" of Høvikodden's architecture.

Visionary architecture

The journal *Byggekunst* is an important source for understanding the context in which Eikvar and Engebretsen were operating. In January 1963, in the middle of the final phase of the architectural competition, Håkon Mjelva reflected in an article entitled "Thoughts at the turn of the year" on two events in the past year "which have given rise to special reflection". This concerned the 'Visionary Architecture' exhibition at MoMA in 1961 and "related in a number of journals in '62", as well as the exhibition of Pier Luigi Nervi's work at A/S Byggtjeneste's premises in January 1962. In his eccentric and artful text, Mjelva criticises "the breathless material pressure of the age" and "the fussing after novelty", and juxtaposes Nervi's concrete architecture, characterised by "a relatively short supply of constructive systems and forms" with the "sea change" heralded by foreign journals with projects in which "the free play of means is more important than achieving, in the broadest sense, a positively functional purpose". The article is illustrated with a grouping of Norwegian industrial works such as the oil tanks from the Esso plant at Slagentangen, cranes from Akers Mek. Verksted A/S in Oslo, high-voltage cable systems at Årdal and Sunndal aluminium plants, as well as Nåvann dam in Mandal and projects from the MoMA exhibition exemplified by Louis Kahn's Center City, Jean-Claude Mazet's Ideal City, Frederick Kiesler's Endless House, William Katavolos's Chemical Architecture, Buckminster Fuller's Geodetic Dome and some of Nervi's completed projects. The text can only be understood as a critique of the projects in MoMA's exhibition, but at the same time it testifies to Mjelva's international orientation and open approach to architecture. As a member of the CIAM-associated group PAGON (Progressive Arkitekters Gruppe, Oslo, Norway) together with colleagues such as Arne Korsmo, Sverre Fehn, Odd Østby, Geir Grung, P.A.M. Mellbye and Christian Norberg-Schulz, Mjelva took the pulse of the international discourse in architecture in the 1950s and 1960s. Since we know that Håkon Mjelva taught the State Architecture Programme while Eikvar and Engebretsen were students, there is reason to believe that his experiences and views played a significant role in shaping the young architecture students' ideological foundation.

The 'Visionary Architecture' exhibition has a very special significance for Eikvar and Engebretsen, and it is symptomatic of a shift in mood in Norwegian architecture. What Mjelva fails to mention in his text is that the exhibition was shown at the same time at the premises of the Oslo Architects' Association on 17–27 January 1963, with Eikvar and Engebretsen responsible for the exhibition.[27] Engebretsen sat on the association's board, was responsible for the association's exhibitions, and introduced 'Visionary Architecture' at the opening. The association had approached MoMA as early as 31 January 1962 with a request to bring the exhibition to Oslo, but it took a year of hard work to make it happen.[28]

In *Aftenposten*'s coverage of the exhibition the day after the opening, under the headline "Fantastic architecture at Oslo exhibition", the journalist

[28] Mjelva, H. 1963: 3–8. The editorial board consisted of Per Cappelen, Kjell Lund and Håkon Mjelva.
[29] MoMA, 1960.

praises the show: "For those who believe along with Baudelaire that imagination is 'the Queen of Qualities', there is an extremely interesting exhibition that opened yesterday..."[29] It continues:

> The whole project is an example of the extent to which the participating architects have broken with prevailing thought. There are also numerous testimonies of a revolution against the 'tyranny of the square'. The architects do not think in right angles.[30]

This is the "exhibition of future architecture" that Eikvar and Engebretsen would refer to in their victory interview a year later. The planning of the exhibition took place in parallel with their work on the competition and provided the architects with ideas and design input for a new art museum at Høvikodden.

The radical artistic project that was erected at Høvikodden in the mid-1960s sought inspiration from many different sources, but found unity in an integrated and total museum which, since its opening in 1968, has manifested itself as one of Scandinavia's most progressive art institutions. The centre's physiognomy testifies to the vital role of architecture in this unique Gesamtkunstwerk and grounds Henie Onstad Kunstsenter in the international architectural discourse of the 1950s and 1960s.

[30] OAF, program 1963. OAF arkiv, boks A: - Foreningsmøteprotokoll 1956-1964.
[31] Brev fra OAFs sekretariat 31.januar 1962. OAF arkiv, boks D: - utstillinger 1931-1978.
[32] Aftenposten 18.januar 1963.
[33] ibid.

Sources:

Fehn, Sverre, Nordisk paviljong ved Biennalen i Venezia, Byggekunst nr.6-1962

Finborud, Lars Mørch, MOT DET TOTALE MUSEUM, Henie Onstad Kunstsenter og tidsbasert kunst 1961-2011, Forlaget Press, 2012

Johnsen, Espen (red): Tandberg, Unni, Etter amerikansk modell?: Eikvar og Engebretsens prøvehus på Henie-Onstad Kunstsenter, i Brytninger: Norsk arkitektur 1945-65, Nasjonalmuseet for kunst, arkitektur og design, 2010

Lending, Mari og Erik Langdalen, Sverre Fehn, Nordic Pavilion, Venice, Lars Müller Publishers/Pax forlag 2021

Mjelva, Håkon, Tanker ved årsskiftet, Byggekunst nr. 1, 1963, s 3-8

Munch, Carsten E., Epoke, NRK Fjernsynet, 1966.

Norberg-Schulz, Christian, «Arkitektur i dag», essay basert på foredrag holdt ved Schweizerisches Werkbunds 50-års jubileum i Zürich 27.oktober 1963. Byggekunst nr.7, 1963

Oslo arkitektforenings arkiv, boks A: - Foreningsmøteprotokoll 1956-1964

Oslo arkitektforenings arkiv, boks D: - utstillinger 1931-1978

Statens Håndverk og Kunstindustriskole i Oslo, årsmeldinger 1954-1955, 1955-1956, 1956-1957, 1957-1958, 1958-1959, 1959-1960

Rudolph, Paul: Tale publisert I "Architecture: The Unending Search," Yale Alumni Magazine 21, no. 8 (May 1958). Gjengitt som "Alumni Day Speech: Yale School of Architecture, February 1958," i Oppositions 4 (1974): 142.

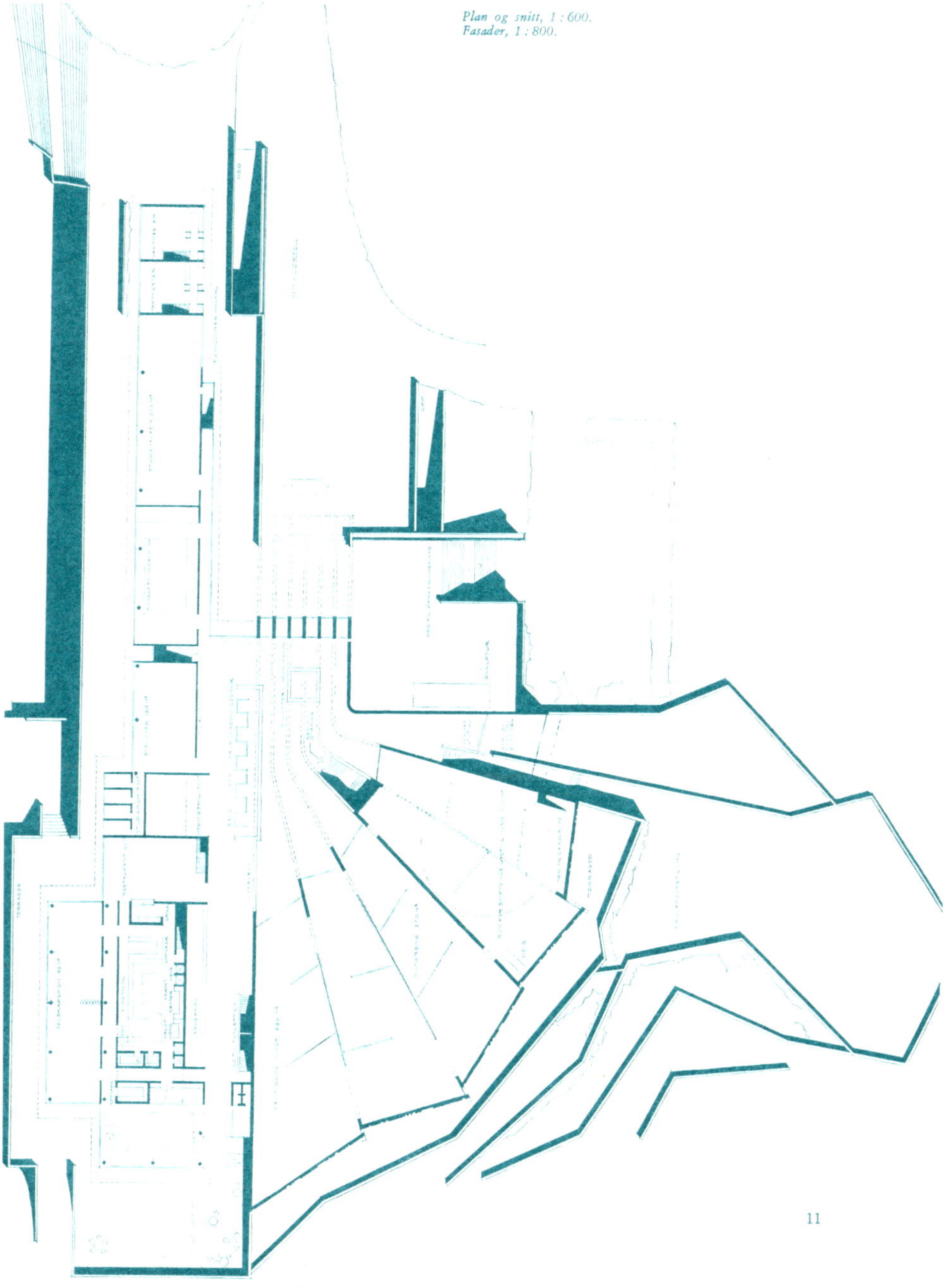

The winning proposal from Eikvar and Engebretsen in its first phase.

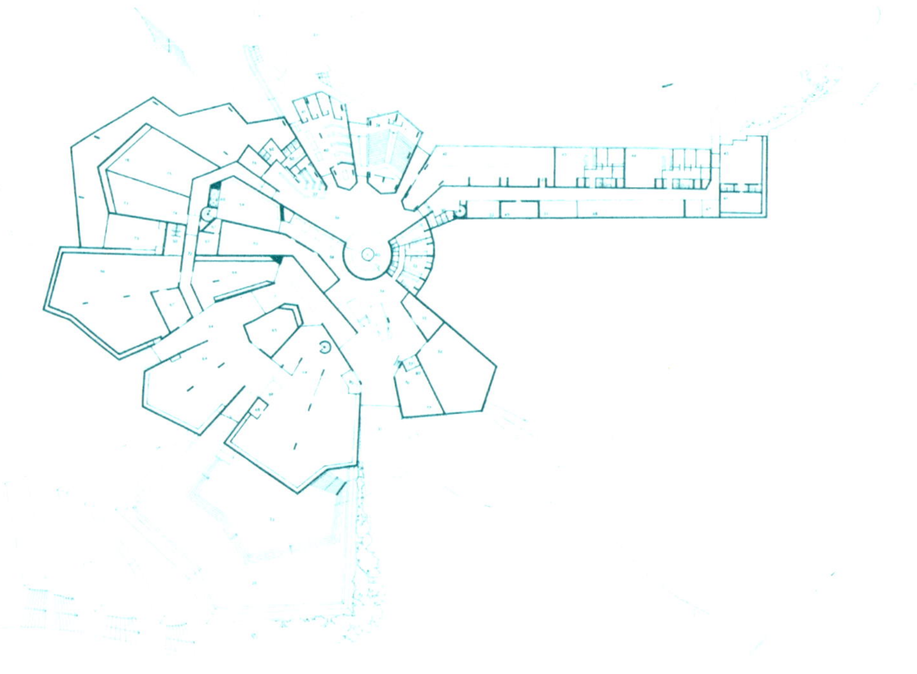

Eikvar and Engebretsen's winning proposal from the second phase of the competition.

TANKER VED ÅRSSKIFTET

Av Håkon Mjelva.

*Over: Louis Kahn, bysentrum fra utstillingen Visjonær Arkitektur.
Under: Oljetanker fra Esso-anlegget på Slagentangen.*

↑

Model

The journal *Byggekunst* is important to understanding the context in which the Norwegian architects were operating. In 1963, Mjelva authored an article in which oil tankers, cable systems and MoMA's groundbreaking 1961 exhibition 'Visionary Architecture' illustrated an artful and eccentric text. Photo: Henie Onstad archive.

←

Building rising up

Sonja Henie had a seat on the museum's committees and held the position of chairwoman of the art centre's board. Photo: Henie Onstad archive

→

Concrete

The art centre was effectively cast and chiselled in natural concrete. Photo: Henie Onstad archive.

←

Collision

Sonja Henie's references came from the entertainment industry, where, over an active lifetime, she built a commercial brand focused on joy, glamour and the body. The art centre's brand was built with the goal of delivering international quality, experimentation and the avant-garde. In this encounter, new discussions emerged. Photo: Henie Onstad archive.

←

The cultural effect

"I think Norway needed something like this - and I think it will have a cultural effect here at home." Niels Onstad in *VG*, 21 June 1967. Photo: Henie Onstad archive.

→

Contrast

It's easy to recognise Sonja Henie's form in the architecture. The white skirt against the sky has its parallel in the ascending white roof. Glass surfaces, hard and smooth as ice, and the dark floor – not unlike her Hollywood productions on black ice. Henie's love of jewellery, glitz and glamour finds its natural counterpart in brass door casings and windowsills. In addition, the central stairwells had red carpets, personally selected and purchased by Sonja on a visit to Hollywood. Photo: Henie Onstad archive.

←

Norwegian design

The centre's furniture design commission was given to Sven Erik Dysthe (1931–2020). Clearly inspired by the aesthetics of the 1960s, together with the ice skating star's accomplishments, he made spinning lounge chairs and pouffes in white imitation leather. Dysthe also made the furniture icon Popcorn to order for Henie and Onstad. The chair has been reproduced for the second time and has become a Norwegian classic. Photo: Simen Ødegaard.

→

Location

Bærum municipality made Høvikodden available for the new museum. The following was written in Budstikka on the occasion of the laying of the foundation stone: "Among those responsible for the project in Bærum municipality, there has never been any doubt about what obligations the local authorities should assume towards an institution such as this. Although in this context the tasks that have fallen on the municipality may have to some extent intensified our expansive village's growing pains, it is quite clear that the cultural institution at Høvikodden puts us in a highly enviable situation!" Photo: Henie Onstad archive.

←

Trophy room

Sonja Henie's trophy room was not included in the initial drafts for the Henie Onstad Kunstsenter. Following feedback from the committees, this was changed so her prizes were given their own place. Photo: Henie Onstad archive.

→

The splits

Sonja Henie wanted large crowds to flock to the centre to experience art and concerts to rival The Beatles. The art centre, on the other hand, took a more experimental path, with Arne Nordheim, John Cage and Stockhausen in the repertoire. In this difference of opinion lie the foundations for making the impossible possible. Photo: Henie Onstad archive.

↑

Extension

Originally the centre had a stone terrace that marked the area going down to the sea. Today this area has evolved into the Great Hall extension, which opened in 1994 – designed by the original architects. Photo: Henie Onstad archive.

→

The long-overdue pier

"Bærum municipality has undertaken to build a pier for seagoing sightseeing traffic, but this is not in the final planning stages yet and will not be completed until next summer." *VG*, 9 August 1968. Photo: Henie Onstad archive.

↓

Photo: Simen Øvergaard / Henie Onstad Kunstsenter.

↑

Music

Before the art centre was ready, music was included as an important interdisciplinary element. Concerts are arranged both inside and outside. Photo: Simen Øvergaard/Henie Onstad Kunstsenter.

←

Rhythm

The public is met by carefully composed glass surfaces when they arrive at the centre. Photo: Simen Øvergaard/Henie Onstad Kunstsenter.

↑

Craftsmanship

The characteristic roof stands in contrast to the hand-chiselled concrete walls. If you study the wall carefully, you can see the skill of each craftsman in the way the chisels have been used. Photo: Henie Onstad archive.

→

Interiors
Sonja Henie steered the process of furnishing the centre. She chose curtains, carpets and furniture. Here she is examining textiles in 1968. Photo: Henie Onstad archive.

←

Hard and soft
The white edges of the roof elements are a soft, curved contrast to the rougher natural concrete of the outer walls. Photo: Henie Onstad archive.

↑

Around and around
The floor of the outdoor amphitheatre is crafted in wood panelling while the benches around it are cast in concrete. Photo: Jacky Penot/Henie Onstad Kunstsenter.

←

Transition
Today an underground passageway runs from the original building to the new Sal Haaken. Outside, a bridge crosses this walkway from the lawn to outdoor amphitheatre. Photo: Simen Øvergaard/Henie Onstad Kunstsenter.

←

Rows and rows
The row of windows along the terrace frames the offices and Cafe Piruetten. Photo: Henie Onstad archive.

TO
NIE
LS

Hotel Tamanaco
Caracas, Venezuela
1.4.1956
11 p.m.

Beloved Niels,

Arrived yesterday p.m. after a lovely trip, I think my 49 skaters were exhausted after a lot of training. Maybe they had a few drinks afterwards. They slept all the way! –

But a quiet, humble troupe! We haven't received costumes, music etc. due to public holidays. I'm hoping for more action tomorrow! Trained tonight, it'll be wonderful. Lots of promotion that I want to send. I arrived in the middle of Easter, which is not good, we open ticket sales tomorrow, four days before we open. I can't train before 7:30 p.m. because of the sun.

Today I have been missing you so much, so much I'm almost sick. – I have a bedroom with living room and an unbeatable porch, life is so empty without you. I think of all the wonderful months we had together. Unfortunately I've not heard a word from you here, but the mail will not be delivered until tomorrow. The post office has been closed for 4 days.

Hope you got your wristwatch, also that your sister was happy with the fur collar. – I must say Caracas is a great city, it is really beautiful here. In 5 more years I think Caracas will be unbeatable! The food so far is inedible, the same "crap" as Cuba.

So a roast for two just as we like it will probably be difficult, everything tastes terrible! There may be places I don't know about.

The weather is glorious, but hot, about 90. So we'll have tarpaulin over the ice until 6.30 p.m..

I have my 3 compressors, which were sent from California, to make the ice perfect, it was necessary. Everything would be wonderful if you were here, beloved, you would like it here!

—

I'm sure you've had a nice Easter, I hope, but hope you missed me a bit!! –

The "pink" champagne that you gave to mother (we brought 5 bottles here, and it tasted good, the caviar too). Darling Niels, where is your journey taking you after Cannes? We hope to be here for 3 weeks. You forgot to give me the address of those people you want me to send tickets to – it's not too late yet! How is your weight?? What a nice time we could have here on the porch (extremely!! – I could fall asleep on your arm).

Monday, April 2, 8 a.m.

Was thinking about you all night, couldn't sleep now we've been apart 10 days, it has been a long 10 days. – Today it's hot, I mustn't get too tanned, everyone down here works in offices, you know, so I have to keep my face out of the sun! – There must be some Negro blood here.

Your car was sent back in the best condition, the upholstery got rubbed down (the way my yellow outfit was), hope it comes back in equally good condition, I'm sure it will. Thank you for lending it to me! Here in Caracas, food is especially expensive, so all the skaters have been given a 15 percent increase in pay.

You are probably now in the mountains, hope you take it easy and rest. Greetings from my mother. Not a word from Leif or the children. Only the dry telegram from Gerd that I sent you. Said to Russer (the jeweller) to write a letter with the watch he sent you, and he said you'd forgotten it and that it was in for repair. Hope you had no trouble with customs. – Darling Niels I love you.

Miss you, hope it won't be too long before we see each other again.

Your Sonja

Hotel Tamanaco
Caracas, Venezuela
April 3 '56

My beloved Niels,

Have received two telegrams, but no letters since you left. – As I told you in my letter yesterday, the post here is hopeless. Mrs Gilbert went to fetch something from the Airport yesterday evening, she took my letter to you and an envelopes with clippings with her, she came back and said no one would take it. She is going out again today and will get them sent, otherwise it takes 8 days to send a letter, about 10 days to Miami. It's completely hopeless, we haven't received the costumes yet, they were sent 2 weeks ago from Miami, not recording, tapes, nothing! It's impossible to figure anything out, they say it's here, but where? Cuba runs at a much better tempo than here, and we said it was hopeless there!

The ice yesterday was crap, they had taken off the sheets that we're covering the rink with at 6 p.m. instead of 7.30 p.m., we had a warm breeze, which is deadly – half the ice was thick frost. The other half was water, and we could feel all the pipes, the 2nd section's leap, "Jeapen" fell to pieces. Goddamn, what a day. It's not been this hot for 20 years, not a breath of wind. –

3pm
Nothing arrived. Cocktail party for the press at 4 today, training at 8. Will continue the letter after training tonight. The cape in the Bullfight number yesterday was hell due to the wind.

3am
Darling, tonight was better, cocktail party was nice, about 200 people, it was nicely set up. AP called at 3.30, they had received a telegram from New York asking whether it was true about my divorce. I said yes. – I'm so tired now, will continue tomorrow. Trained from 8–2.30 a.m.. The skaters will train until

4 a.m.. Half of the costumes came tonight, none of mine – I skated nicely tonight.

The president is coming to the opening night. Opened ticket sales today at 12. First hour $3,500. Took in $15,000 today. We're only selling the opening night. Tomorrow we're selling 2 days in advance. Colossal advertising, I've never had so many press people, photographers, television, 5 newsreel cameras, they were killing me with questions. Divorce no. 1 which came out a few hours before the cocktail party.

April 4

7 a.m.

Couldn't sleep tonight, you know I've got my head full, also thinking about you so much and miss you so much darling Niels. I'm in good shape, have never been better than last night, it's hard to skate here. Tonight we start at 6, will go through the show with the orchestra, hope we get the rest of the costumes during the day. We'll be at it all night, there'll no doubt be both "golden and diamond" hours – the Bullfight number will be the best in the show.

The press asked only about my divorce at the cocktail party and how much money I had, what my jewellery costs. You've never heard such idiotic questions.

Everyone nervous about the opening. Got the pipes on the ice fixed, some sand had got inside them so it had to be blown out, sloppy work. If my engineer who has been with me since 1936 wasn't here (this would never have happened to him) I would never have got it right (you met him in Miami), he is 70 years old, now works only for me when I have these difficult jobs.

3 a.m.

Got home now from dress rehearsal. The music is beyond all criticism. Got the costumes tonight at 8. If it goes well tomorrow, it's only by sheer good luck. All wrong! The acrobats I had at the Roxy have not got the ladder or their costumes, they say it will be here tomorrow afternoon. – Say no more!

Regards
Your Sonja

Love you, and that is basically what matters most. You are everything in my life, hope we can be as happy forever as we have been for the rest of our lives.

Your puss.

→

Pirouette

Look carefully and you'll notice that the building's stairs take the same pirouette form as the entrance. Photo: Henie Onstad archive.

←

Fan

The centre's original exhibition halls were named Prisma after the playfulness that occurred when light broke through the centre's multifaceted forms and roof. Photo: Henie Onstad archive.

→

Tour

Sonja Henie gave King Olav a tour of the collection during the opening. Photo: Henie Onstad archive.

←

Reflection

The donors' ambition to create a living art centre permitted space for an artistic programme that could push the boundaries. Photo: Simen Øvergaard/ Henie Onstad Kunstsenter. © Per Inge Bjørlo/BONO 2021.

↑

Focal point

Sonja Henie and Niels Onstad on the stage of the centre's amphitheatre in 1968. Photo: Henie Onstad archive.

↑

The stairs

"I want light!" said Sonja Henie. So simple and so exacting. This one sentence was her brief to the Swiss designer Siegfried Odermatt (1926–) who created the centre's first logo, formed by the two central flights of stairs in the building. Photo: Henie Onstad archive .

Swift as a bird, Sonja died in the air, high above the land she conquered. The queen of ice was on her way home. An ambassador for her country, the likes of which we had never before seen. She belonged to no one, but was everyone's property, and therein lay the key to her loneliness. She was more human than many people I have met. Generous in big ways – this is a fact – but also in small and intimate ways, because it came so simply, so naturally. Sonja stayed faithful to the nature of her being, without betraying her origins, which she herself exalted above all else. She was dutiful in her focus, which was subject to her force of will, and she smiled the smile of a young girl all her life.

In deep reverence I wish to thank Sonja for what she was, for what she gave. She couldn't help but win, and no one knows the price she paid for it. It is inconceivable that Sonja is no longer with us, the whole sparkling magnificence of the woman who lifted everything and everyone towards the light. But wherever she is, some place or other, because maybe there is something higher, much bigger – Sonja will get her little ice rink – no, she will get the biggest one, and then it will come, the White Swan, sailing over the crystals of ice in the golden glow of an eternal sun.

The great fairy tale is over. But as it goes with fairy tales, if it's good, well, then it lives forevermore, as the Norwegian artist Jakob Weidemann (1923–2001) said when he spoke in memory of Sonja Henie at her funeral at Haslum, 17 October 1969 .

Paris 1. november 1969.

Det var et brutalt sjokk for oss da vi mandag morgen 13. oktober gjennom radioen fikk høre at Sonja var død aftenen før. Vi trodde at hun og Niels var lykkelig og vel i Lissabon -

Fredagen før traff vi dem utenfor hotellet deres i Fbg. St.Honoré smilende og glade i morgensolen. Stor omfavnelse. Og om kvelden hadde vi dinner sammen på Fouquet, Sonja og Niels og Hans og jeg. Det var en av de særdeles hyggelige aftener - som når gode venner treffes igjen og har masse å snakke om: muséet deres, utstillingsplaner, kunst, mat og alt mulig. Sonja og jeg ertet våre menn som var så altfor glad i mat.

Og vi bestemte oss til å treffes mye oftere herefter - for livet er så kort - - -

Det siste bilde jeg har i erindringen av den kvelden er Sonja og Niels, arm i arm på Champs-Elysées, som vinket efter oss i taxien, og vi til dem så lenge vi kunde øyne dem.

Da jeg senere fikk vite av Niels at både Sonja selv og han visste hvor syk hun var, ble min beundring enda større enn den allerede var, over en slik fantastisk viljestyrke til inntil det aller siste å gjennomføre sitt liv fullt ut positivt.

Hele hennes liv var positivt.
Alt hun har gjort for sin egen kunst og senere for andres kunst, og sist men ikke minst for sitt land, er et fantastisk eksempel på viljestyrke, mot og disiplin:

Sonja på skøytebanen i Frognerkilen - 11 år
Sonja på veldedighetsbasar på Bristol - 14 år
Det er glimt jeg husker fra min egen barndom da vi jentunger stod beundrende i ærbødig avstand for å få et glimt av henne.

Da jeg senere giftet meg i Dresden fant jeg Sonja igjen: stort bilde av Sonja på skøytebanen på veggen i min manns atelier. Han var allerede da stor beundrer av Sonja Henie.

Mange år senere - i 1956, tror jeg, besøkte Sonja oss i Paris sammen med Niels. Sonja sa ærlig: "Det er Niels som skjønner seg på kunst, ikke jeg!" hvorpå hun bomsikkert stilet rett på de beste bildene til Hans.

Sonja har imponert meg enormt fordi hun er et av de meget sjeldne mennesker som fra først til sist har gjort maksimum ut av sitt liv.

Anna Eva Bergman.

↑
Anna Eva Bergman's letter to Henie Onstad Kunstsenter following news of Sonja Henie's death.

1912
Born 8 April in Oslo.

1918–23
Starts skating at Frogner Stadium. From the age of nine she holds performances during intervals at the stadium's big competitions.

1924
At eleven years old, she participates for the first time in major competitions: the world championship in Oslo and the Olympics in Chamonix.

1925
Wins her first Norwegian championship (Moss) and starts traveling around the country to perform shows.

1926
Wins two Norwegian championships (Tønsberg), solo and in a pair with Arne Lie.

1927
Wins Norwegian championship (Oslo), solo and pair skating with Arne Lie, as well as the world championship (Oslo) and begins performing internationally. Stars in her first film, *Syv dager for Elisabeth* (directed by Leif Sinding).

1928
Wins world championships (London), Olympics (St. Moritz) and Norwegian championships (Sandefjord) solo and in a pair with Arne Lie.

1929
Wins world championships (Budapest) and Norwegian championships (Lillehammer).

1930
Winner of the world championships (New York). This is her first time in America and after the competition she embarks on a tour of performances around the United States and Canada.

1931
Wins the world championships (Berlin) and European championships (St. Moritz).

1936
Wins the world championships (Paris), the European championships (Berlin) and the Olympics (Garmisch-Partenkirchen). Travels to Hollywood to become a movie star and works professionally with travelling skating shows. Signs a major contract with Fox and shoots *One in a Million* – the world's most watched film of the year.

1938
Publishes the autobiography *My Life's Adventures*.

1937–49
Shoots eleven films in Hollywood and at the same time goes on tour every year with major ice shows around the United States. Marries Dan Topping 1940–1946 and then Winthrop Gardiner 1949–1956. Publishes the autobiography *Wings on My Feet* in 1940.

1952
Tours in Cuba and Canada, among other places.

1953–55
Publishes the autobiography *My Life's Adventures* with a new narrative.

Tour of Europe. Returns to Oslo with a big ice show at Jordal Arena. The show sets a record and is seen by 350,000 people. Repeats the success in 1955.

1956
Tour of South America. Marries Niels Onstad 1956–1969 and spends more time in Norway (Landøya). Retires from touring. Hones her interest in art and begins the work of building a large art collection in parallel with her husband's collection.

1958
Shoots her last film *Hello London* for Regal film.

1961
Sonja Henie and Niels Onstad donate their art collections and funds to build a magnificent building and an operating fund for a foundation bearing their name. Their gift is the largest private donation in Norway.

1968
Henie Onstad Art Center opens. It is one of the Nordic region's foremost art centres for modern art.

1969
Sonja Henie dies of leukaemia on 12 October on a flight from Paris to Oslo.

Solskulptur by Arnold Haukeland (1920–1983) is massive and monumental. The sculpture was erected by Sonja Henie's last husband Niels Onstad in her memory, following her sudden death on a flight home from Paris in 1969. The base is yellow and is mounted on what was originally a fully functioning piece of machinery. It was made to turn on its own axis, like a pirouette or beam of light. But *Solskulptur* turned only briefly. It is said that gravity was too much for it. The small underground electric motor was controlled by one gear. The huge pressure from the sculpture's pirouette snapped the engine bracket and the mechanics fell apart. But even motionless, the sculpture is just as impressive. It stands firm in the park, paused in its own round dance. In form and as a monument, it is a clear landmark. Sonja Henie is buried in this same park, directly opposite the art centre she got built with Niels Onstad. Photo: Mathilde N. Thafvelin / Henie Onstad Kunstsenter.